C902534142

This book
belongs to

....

D1341674

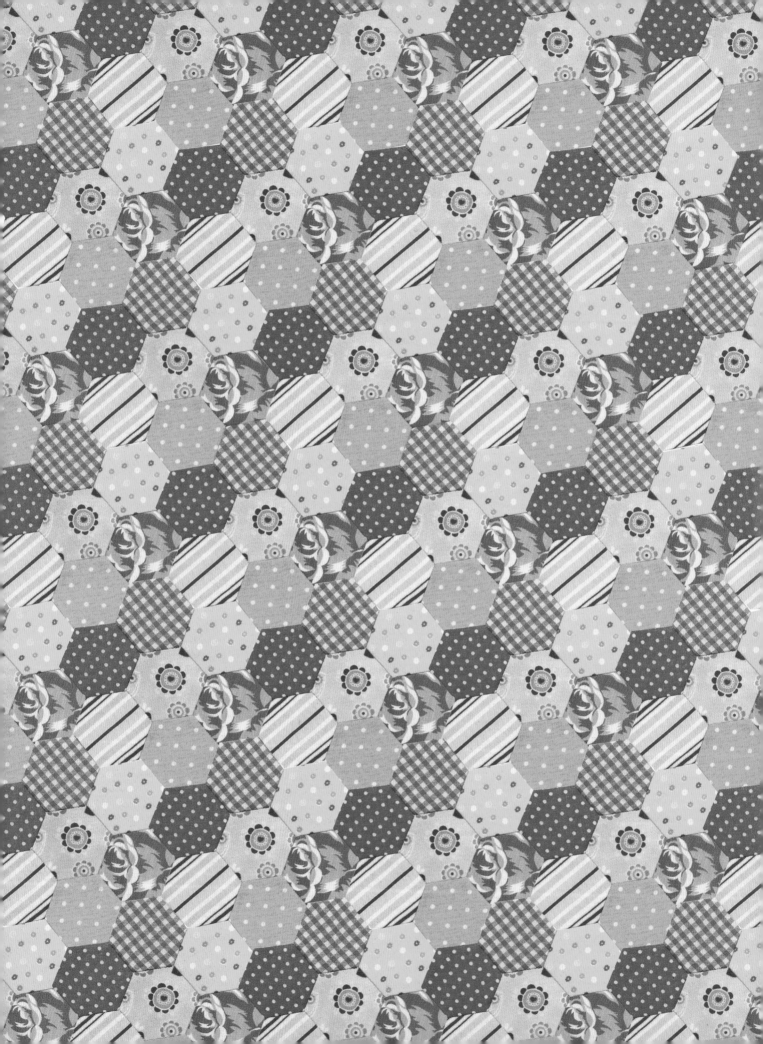

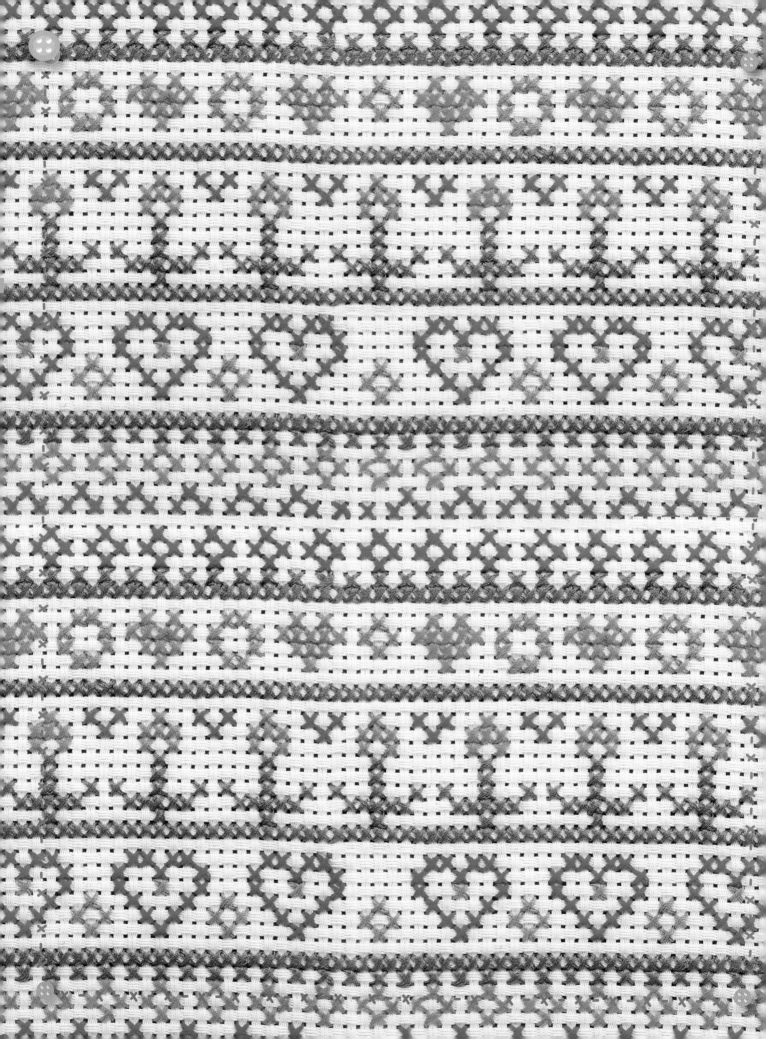

Stitch
-by-
Stitch

JANE BULL

Penguin Random House

DESIGN AND TEXT Jane Bull
PHOTOGRAPHER Andy Crawford
SENIOR EDITOR Carrie Love
EDITORS Alexander Cox, Lee Wilson
DESIGNERS Charlotte Bull, Lauren Rosier
JACKET DESIGNER Amy Keast
PRE-PRODUCTION EDITOR Dragana Puvacic
PRODUCTION CONTROLLER Inderjit Bhullar
CREATIVE DIRECTOR Jane Bull
CATEGORY PUBLISHER Mary Ling

First published in hardback in
Great Britain in 2012
This paperback edition published in 2016 by
Dorling Kindersley Limited
80 Strand, London WC2R 0RL

Copyright © 2012 Dorling Kindersley Limited
A Penguin Random House Company
Copyright © 2012 Jane Bull
10 9 8 7 6 5 4 3 2 1
001–181751–Jul/16

All rights reserved.
No part of this publication may be reproduced,
stored in or introduced into a retrieval system,
or transmitted, in any form, or by any means
(electronic, mechanical, photocopying, recording,
or otherwise), without the prior written
permission of the copyright owner.

A CIP catalogue record for this book
is available from the British Library.
ISBN: 978-0-2412-5731-9

Printed and bound in China

All images © Dorling Kindersley Limited
For further information see: www.dkimages.com

A WORLD OF IDEAS:
SEE ALL THERE IS TO KNOW
www.dk.com

This book's for my
needlecraft teacher
Barbara Owen
(who's also my mum).

Crochet

Embroidery

Stitch-by-Stitch

is all about needlecraft,
and introduces beginners to embroidery,
crochet, patchwork, appliqué, knitting,
and needlepoint. It teaches basic
techniques and then takes them a step
further, showing how to use these skills
to create fun and beautiful projects,
revitalizing the crafts our grandmothers
took for granted and bringing them
up to date.

Patchwork

Knitting

Needlepoint

Appliqué

Contents

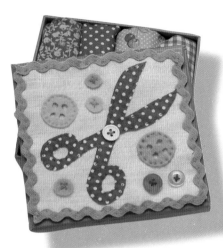

Keep your sewing essentials in little boxes.

SOFT-TOY FILLING is used for stuffing projects such as patchwork balls, cushions, and knitted dolls. It is a lightweight material that gives an even stuffing.

FELT is available in lots of colours. It's easy to cut into small shapes and is a useful backing material.

Felt is perfect for projects because the edges don't fray.

RIBBONS and braids are great for decorating projects, so keep a selection in your sewing box.

Keep to hand

Here is a selection of equipment and materials that will come in handy when making the projects in this book.

Self-covering DIY buttons can be bought in craft shops.

Safety pins to make brooches

Brightly coloured buttons

PINKING SHEARS are special scissors with zig-zag-shaped blades that make a shape when cutting fabric. The zig-zag edge prevents the material from fraying.

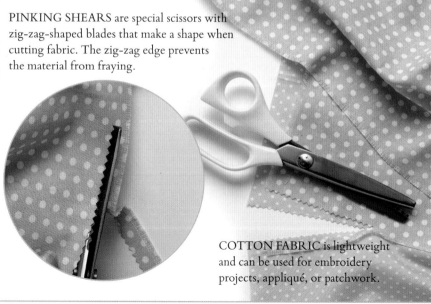

COTTON FABRIC is lightweight and can be used for embroidery projects, appliqué, or patchwork.

A button box

Sewing basics

All the projects in Stitch-by-Stitch will need a handy kit like this, as well as the materials and equipment required for a particular technique. You will also need to know some basic sewing skills to complete the projects.

Sewing box

You can buy a sewing box to store all your sewing equipment and materials, but why not make one out of a shoebox instead?

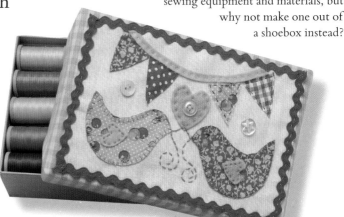

Handy tip

Remember to keep this kit with you when making the projects in this book.

Thread

It's handy to have a selection of sewing threads in different colours so you can match them to the fabrics you use. Needle threaders are useful.

Needles

Sewing needles are usually thin with either a small eye or a long thin eye. Keep a selection of needles in a needle case.

Pins

You'll need pins in a lot of the sewing projects. A pincushion keeps your pins safe and always at hand. Glass-headed pins are pretty and easy to see when dropped.

SEWING THREAD

NEEDLE THREADER

EMBROIDERY SCISSORS

NEEDLE CASE

PIN CUSHION

DRESSMAKERS' SCISSORS

THIMBLE

TAPE MEASURE

Scissors

It helps to have good sharp scissors and the right ones for the job. Embroidery scissors are best for snipping threads and dressmakers' scissors are best for cutting larger pieces of fabric.

Thimble

You wear a thimble on the middle finger of the hand that is holding the needle. It is used to push the needle through the fabric and stops your finger from getting sore.

Tape measure

Some projects will have thread, fabric, and yarn that need accurate measuring.

Threading a needle

Threading a needle can be difficult. A needle with a larger eye will make it easier or use a needle threader. Use sharp scissors to cut the thread.

Thread length?

If you work with thread that is too long it will get tangled, slowing you down. Cut a piece of thread roughly the length from your fingers to your elbow.

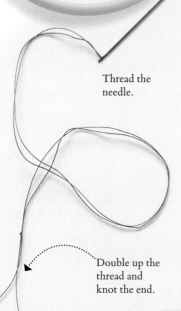

Thread the needle.

Double up the thread and knot the end.

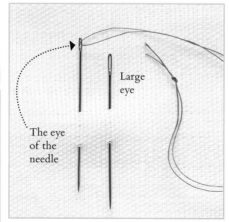

Large eye

The eye of the needle

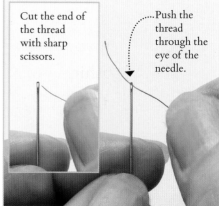

Cut the end of the thread with sharp scissors.

Push the thread through the eye of the needle.

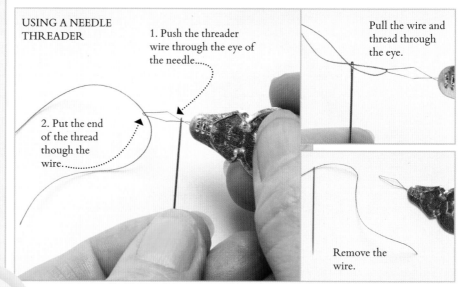

USING A NEEDLE THREADER

1. Push the threader wire through the eye of the needle....

2. Put the end of the thread though the wire.

Pull the wire and thread through the eye.

Remove the wire.

Sewing on a button

1

First secure the thread in the fabric. Then put the button onto the needle and drop it down the thread.

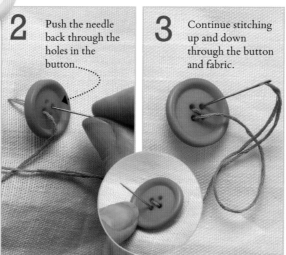

2 Push the needle back through the holes in the button.

3 Continue stitching up and down through the button and fabric.

4 To secure the button bring the thread up under the button.

Sew backwards and forwards behind the button, then cut the thread.

Sewing stitches

Here are the stitches that are used for the projects. They all have a different job to do when you are joining fabric together for cushions, bags, and patchwork pieces.

How to start and finish

Begin stitching with a knot at the end of the thread. To end a row of stitches, make a tiny stitch, but do not pull it tight. Bring the thread back up through the loop and pull tight. Do this once more in the same spot, then cut the thread.

Running stitch

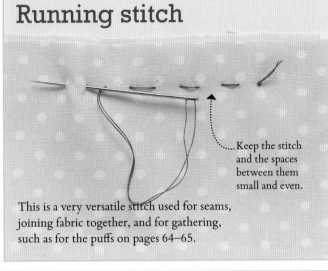

....Keep the stitch and the spaces between them small and even.

This is a very versatile stitch used for seams, joining fabric together, and for gathering, such as for the puffs on pages 64–65.

Back stitch

Make the stitch then bring ..... the needle back to the place where the last stitch is finished.

This is the strongest stitch. It makes a continuous line of stitches so it is best for joining two pieces of fabric securely, like the sides of a bag.

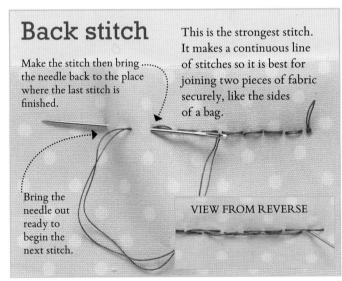

Bring the needle out ready to begin the next stitch.

VIEW FROM REVERSE

Tacking stitch

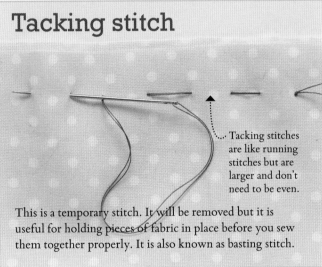

Tacking stitches are like running stitches but are larger and don't need to be even.

This is a temporary stitch. It will be removed but it is useful for holding pieces of fabric in place before you sew them together properly. It is also known as basting stitch.

Overstitch

Insert the needle diagonally from the back of the fabric..

Pick up only two or three threads of fabric.

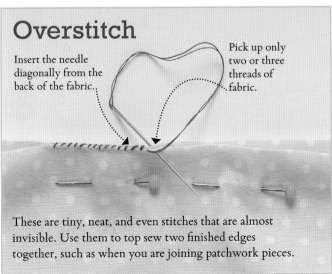

These are tiny, neat, and even stitches that are almost invisible. Use them to top sew two finished edges together, such as when you are joining patchwork pieces.

Slip stitch

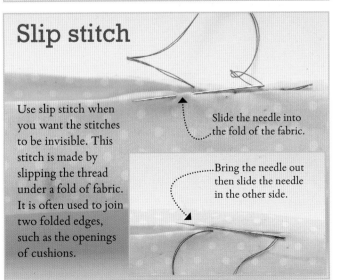

Slide the needle into the fold of the fabric.

Use slip stitch when you want the stitches to be invisible. This stitch is made by slipping the thread under a fold of fabric. It is often used to join two folded edges, such as the openings of cushions.

....Bring the needle out then slide the needle in the other side.

Embroidery

In needlework, embroidery is the handicraft of decorating fabric or other materials with a needle and thread. With a variety of stitches it's possible to create beautiful pictures and patterns.

8-count Binca

Plain-weave fabric

Any kind of fabric can be used for embroidery stitches. Here are examples of cotton, linen, and felt. These fabrics are ideal for freestyle embroidery.

Cotton and linen fabric

Cotton gingham

Embroidery needle

Tapestry needle

Felt

Even-weave fabric

These fabrics are designed especially for embroidery. Woven from cotton, the square mesh produces regular stitches. They are gauged by the count or number of threads to every 2.5cm (1in). The more threads, the finer the fabric.

14-count Aida cloth

13cm (5in) hoop

Embroidery thread

8cm (3in) hoop

Needles and threads

The two types of needle used in the projects are embroidery for fine fabric and tapestry.

Embroidery threads are made up of six strands which can be separated. Finer fabric will require fewer strands.

Hoops

Embroidery hoops are round frames that come in small and large sizes. Flimsy fabric can be clamped tight so it's easier to work on.

Designs on even-weave fabric

Here is an example to show how the different counted thread affects the design. Notice how the same motif, using the same amount of stitches, changes size.

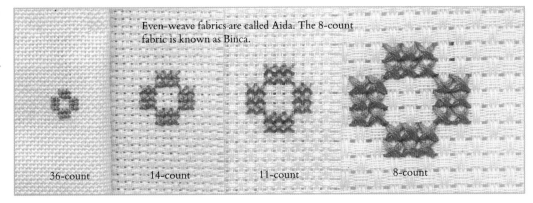

Even-weave fabrics are called Aida. The 8-count fabric is known as Binca.

36-count   14-count   11-count   8-count

Transferring designs

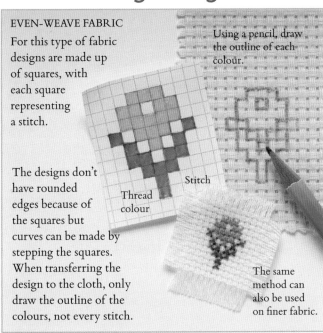

EVEN-WEAVE FABRIC

For this type of fabric designs are made up of squares, with each square representing a stitch.

The designs don't have rounded edges because of the squares but curves can be made by stepping the squares. When transferring the design to the cloth, only draw the outline of the colours, not every stitch.

Using a pencil, draw the outline of each colour.

Thread colour

Stitch

The same method can also be used on finer fabric.

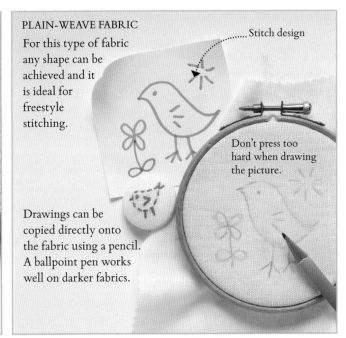

PLAIN-WEAVE FABRIC

For this type of fabric any shape can be achieved and it is ideal for freestyle stitching.

Drawings can be copied directly onto the fabric using a pencil. A ballpoint pen works well on darker fabrics.

Stitch design

Don't press too hard when drawing the picture.

How to use a hoop

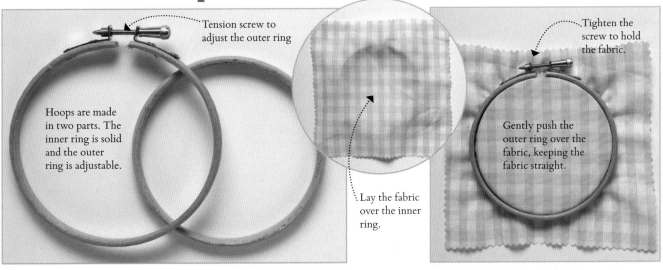

Tension screw to adjust the outer ring

Hoops are made in two parts. The inner ring is solid and the outer ring is adjustable.

Lay the fabric over the inner ring.

Tighten the screw to hold the fabric.

Gently push the outer ring over the fabric, keeping the fabric straight.

Stitches gallery

Running stitch

This stitch makes a dashed line. The stitches can vary in length depending on the effect you want.

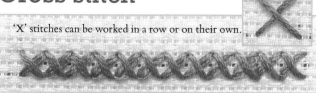

Make stitches by bringing the needle in and out....

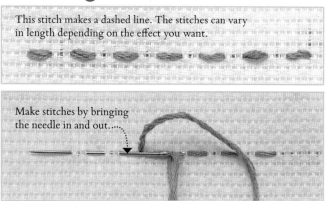

Back stitch

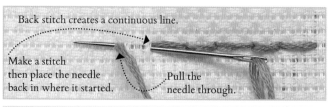

Back stitch creates a continuous line.

Make a stitch then place the needle back in where it started.

Pull the needle through.

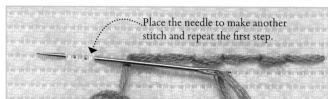

Place the needle to make another stitch and repeat the first step.

Cross stitch

'X' stitches can be worked in a row or on their own.

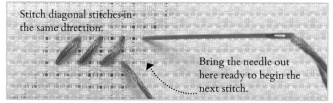

Stitch diagonal stitches in the same direction.

Bring the needle out here ready to begin the next stitch.

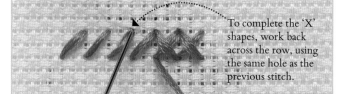

To complete the 'X' shapes, work back across the row, using the same hole as the previous stitch.

Blanket stitch

This stitch is perfect for edging projects and for decoration.

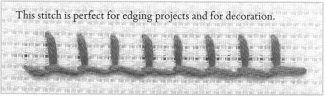

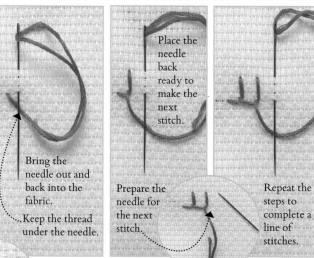

Place the needle back ready to make the next stitch.

Bring the needle out and back into the fabric.

Keep the thread under the needle.

Prepare the needle for the next stitch.

Repeat the steps to complete a line of stitches.

Chain stitch

A decorative stitch with a chain effect

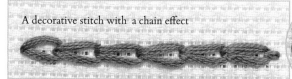

Single chains can look like leaves or petals.

Bring the needle out and then back next to where it came out......

Pull the thread through until it forms a loop.

Bring the needle back up just inside the loop.

Place the needle back next to where it came out.

Make a new loop and repeat the steps to continue making a chain.

Crown stitch

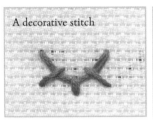

A decorative stitch

Bring the thread round to form a loose stitch.

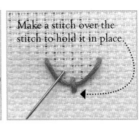

Make a stitch over the stitch to hold it in place.

Continue making stitches...

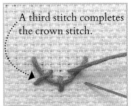

A third stitch completes the crown stitch.

French knot

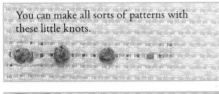

You can make all sorts of patterns with these little knots.

Wind the thread twice around the needle.

Push the needle back in close to the first stitch.

Pull the needle through to form the knot.

Handy tip

Cut a length of thread that is about the length from your fingertips to your elbow to avoid tangles and knots in the thread.

Threading a needle

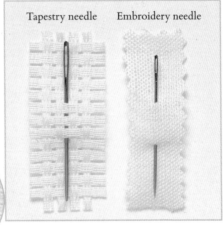

Tapestry needle   Embroidery needle

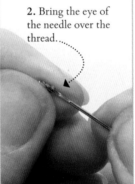

Separate out the six strands.

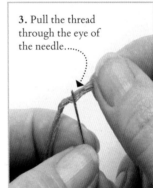

To separate the six strands, hold three strands with one hand and slide the other hand down the length of the thread.

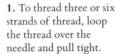

1. To thread three or six strands of thread, loop the thread over the needle and pull tight.

2. Bring the eye of the needle over the thread.

3. Pull the thread through the eye of the needle.

Starting and stopping

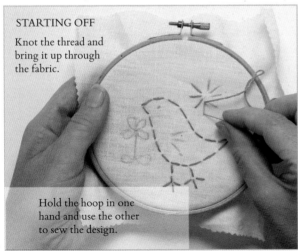

STARTING OFF

Knot the thread and bring it up through the fabric.

Hold the hoop in one hand and use the other to sew the design.

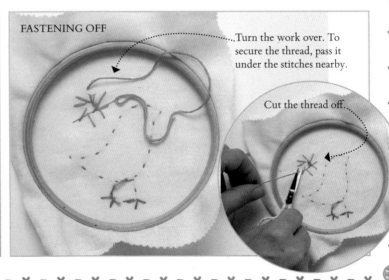

FASTENING OFF

Turn the work over. To secure the thread, pass it under the stitches nearby.

Cut the thread off.

Running stitch...

Single chain stitch

Garden bird

Doodles make great buttons (see page 34).

Use a running stitch to follow the outline of your doodle.

Kitty cat

Add colour to your doodles by using coloured thread.

Use different sizes of embroidery hoop.

Embroidery hoops can be used as picture frames. Just leave your work in place and on the reverse gather up the fabric and tape it in place.

Love hearts

Fireworks

Stitching doodles
A great way
to use your doodles is to recreate them in stitches. Even simple scribbles when stitched can be made into something special.

Happy cloud

Choose fabric that is lightweight and has a loose weave, such as this cotton.

How to stitch a doodle

When you've chosen your doodle, either copy it by drawing it directly onto the fabric with a pencil, or transfer it using tracing paper (see page 51).

You will need

- Your doodles
- Embroidery hoop
- Fabric cotton or linen • Embroidery threads • Embroidery needle • Pencil
- Sewing needle and thread

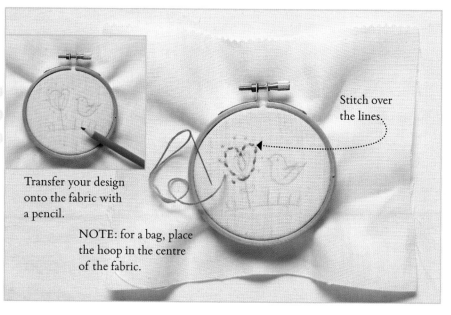

Transfer your design onto the fabric with a pencil.

NOTE: for a bag, place the hoop in the centre of the fabric.

Stitch over the lines.

Continue stitching ...

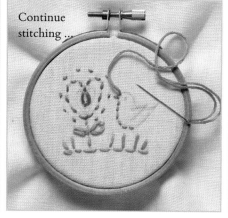

Remove the hoop.

How to make a bag

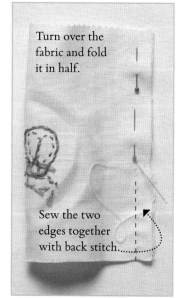

Turn over the fabric and fold it in half.

Sew the two edges together with back stitch.

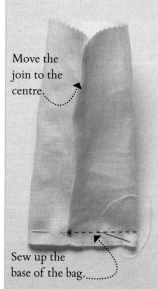

Move the join to the centre.

Sew up the base of the bag.

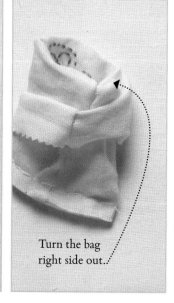

Turn the bag right side out.

The finished design will appear on the front.

Gift bags

If you are looking for something to wrap a gift in try popping it into one of these little bags and finish it off with a ribbon ... now you have two gifts in one!

For sweet smells fill with dried lavender.

Just by using simple stitches like blanket stitch, chain stitch, and straight stitch you can make really colourful designs.

Felt flowers

To make a bunch of flowers save all those pretty scraps of felt and transform them into bright and cheery blooms. Play with the colours of the felt and thread for dazzling effects.

Attaching a pin to the back of the flower makes a charming brooch.

You will need

- Colourful felt scraps
- Embroidery thread
- Embroidery needle

Small lengths of embroidery thread

Save small pieces of felt for projects like this.

Flower templates

Place tracing paper on top of these shapes and trace over them with pencil. Transfer the design onto thin card. Cut out the card and use the shapes for the felt flower.

See page 120 for transferring designs.

How to stitch a flower

To make a flower shape first lay the template on a piece of felt. Carefully draw around the edge of the card and around the centre. This will be a guide to show you where to start the flower centre.

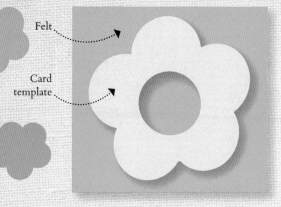

Felt

Card template

You will need

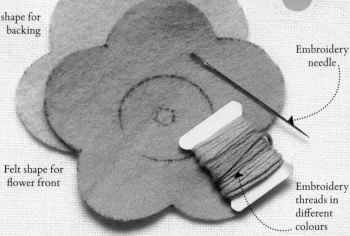

Felt shape for backing

Embroidery needle

Felt shape for flower front

Embroidery threads in different colours

1 Start stitching the centre of the flower.

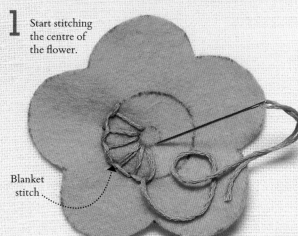

Blanket stitch

2

Single chain stitch

Use straight stitches beside the chain stitch.

3 Sew the front and back pieces together.

Running stitch

4

Safety pin

Attach a safety pin by sewing it to the back of the flower.

Your flower embroidery can be used to cover buttons too. See how on pages 34–35.

Brighten up your T-shirts, jackets, and jeans with colourful stitches.

Sewing flowers on your clothes

Use the flower template to draw out the area you want to sew. Then simply follow the steps for the felt flowers.

Choose where you want the stitching to go and mark it out in the same way as on the felt.

Flower patch

Use the flowers as patches – sew them on to clothes and bags.

....Pin a flower to the garment.

Sew the flower in position using a running stitch.

Decorated beany hat

You will need

Patterned
cotton fabric

Buttons
and ribbons

Embroidery
thread

YOU WILL ALSO NEED
• Embroidery hoop, large enough to fit your template • Embroidery needle • Soft-toy stuffing

Pretty birdies

Collect up pieces of patterned fabric to create these cute little birds. Use embroidery stitches to give the birds features and have fun with the fabric print, following the flower shapes to create a really special effect.

How to make a bird

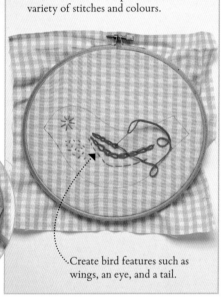

Place the fabric in the hoop.

Draw around the card shape with a pencil.

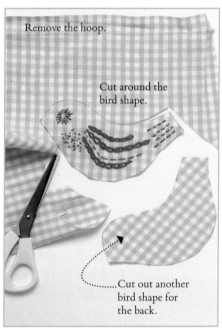

Decorate the bird shape with a variety of stitches and colours.

Create bird features such as wings, an eye, and a tail.

Remove the hoop.

Cut around the bird shape.

Cut out another bird shape for the back.

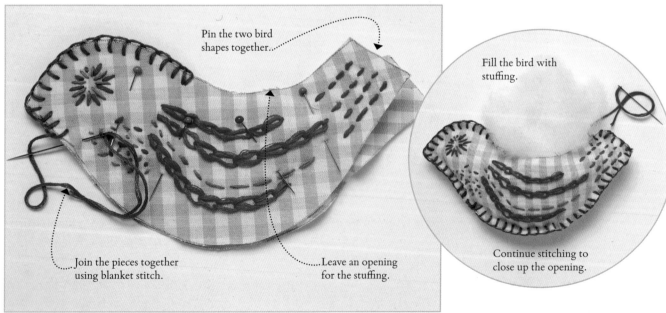

Pin the two bird shapes together...

Fill the bird with stuffing.

Join the pieces together using blanket stitch.

Leave an opening for the stuffing.

Continue stitching to close up the opening.

Handy tip

Why not use the design on the patterned fabric to guide your stitches. Follow the outline of the petals and add chain-stitch leaves using threads in contrasting colours. Finish off with buttons for eyes.

Hanging pretty

To make hanging birds, cut a length of ribbon 20cm (8in). Fold it in half and sew it to the bird, adding a button for extra decoration.

Gingham cross stitch

Gingham is a type of cotton fabric with a check design. The checks come in an array of colours and different sizes; from tiny squares to huge ones. Make the most of this ready-made pattern to try out your cross-stitch.

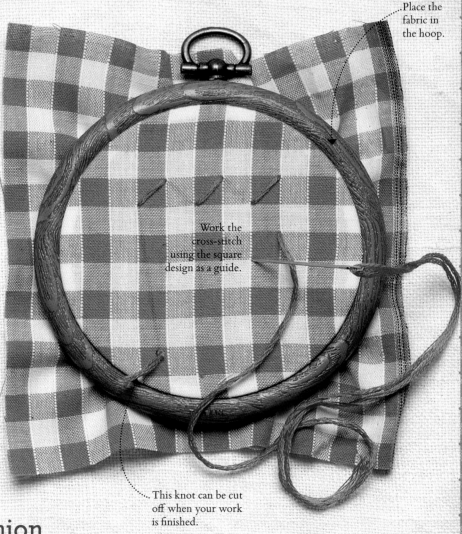

Place the fabric in the hoop.

Work the cross-stitch using the square design as a guide.

This knot can be cut off when your work is finished.

You will need

- Gingham fabric • Fabric for back • Embroidery hoop • Embroidery needle and thread • Soft-toy filling • Sewing needle and thread

How to make a cushion

1

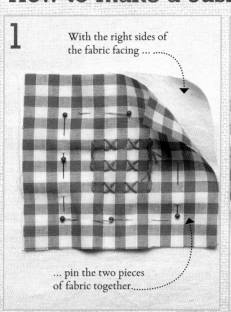

With the right sides of the fabric facing …

… pin the two pieces of fabric together.

2

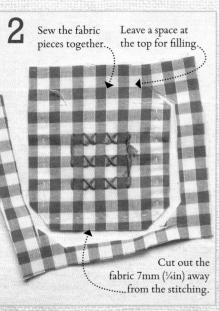

Sew the fabric pieces together.

Leave a space at the top for filling.

Cut out the fabric 7mm (¼in) away from the stitching.

3

Fill the cushion case, but don't overfill.

Turn the cushion case right-side out.

Using a sewing needle and thread, carefully sew the opening together.

Simple sampler

Try out your skills with a sampler. Traditionally, samplers were a way to practice your skills at embroidery. Here is an easy design of hearts and flowers to start on.

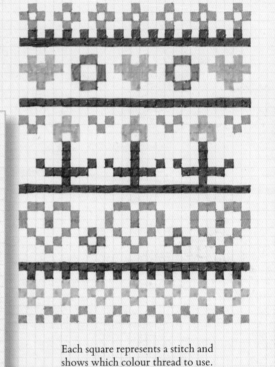

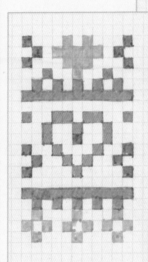

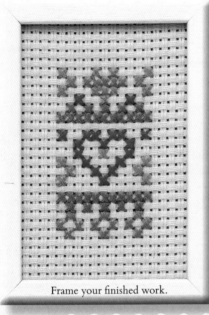

Frame your finished work.

Each square represents a stitch and shows which colour thread to use.

You will need

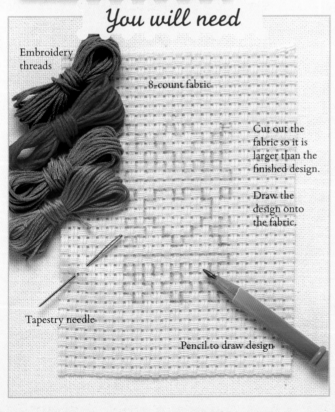

Embroidery threads

8-count fabric

Cut out the fabric so it is larger than the finished design.

Draw the design onto the fabric.

Tapestry needle

Pencil to draw design

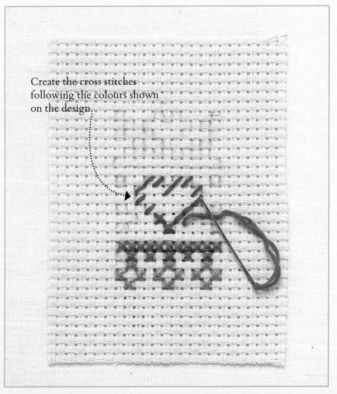

Create the cross stitches following the colours shown on the design.

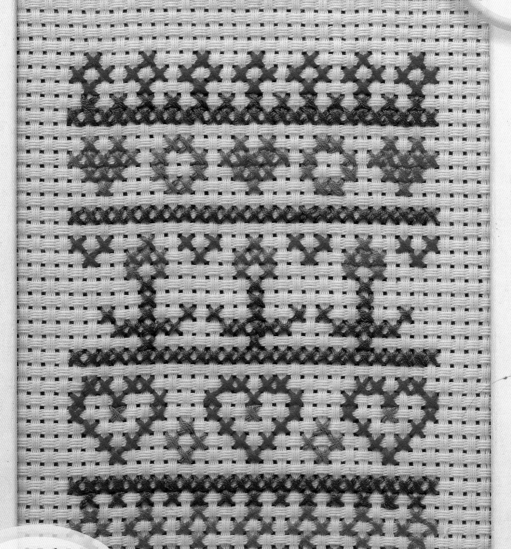

Good gifts

These homemade samplers make perfect gifts. Frame and attach some ribbon for hanging.

Make it larger

Use the alternative template to create a larger sampler. Remember it's not necessary to draw the entire design onto the fabric; the first few rows will help as a guide.

See pages 122–123 for templates.

Pictures in stitches

Big and small You can make the same picture in a different size by using a different counted-thread fabric.

You will need
• 8-count and 14-count cross-stitch fabric • Embroidery needle and thread

Make a picture

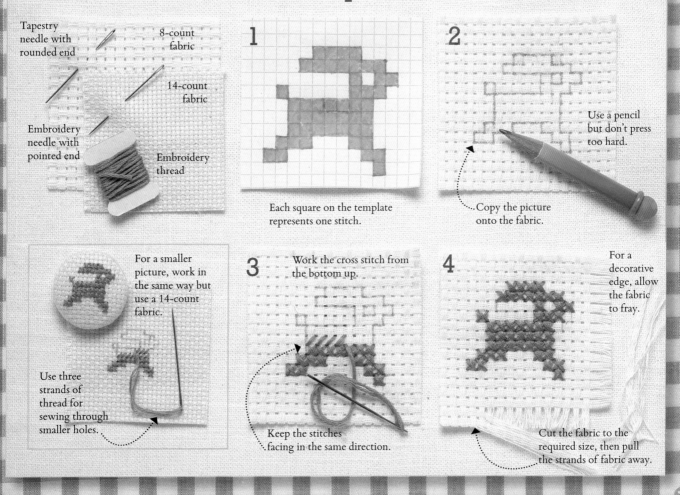

Tapestry needle with rounded end

8-count fabric

14-count fabric

Embroidery needle with pointed end

Embroidery thread

1 Each square on the template represents one stitch.

2 Use a pencil but don't press too hard.

Copy the picture onto the fabric.

For a smaller picture, work in the same way but use a 14-count fabric.

Use three strands of thread for sewing through smaller holes.

3 Work the cross stitch from the bottom up.

Keep the stitches facing in the same direction.

4 For a decorative edge, allow the fabric to fray.

Cut the fabric to the required size, then pull the strands of fabric away.

See pages 34–35 for making buttons.

DIY key fob from craft shop

Glue your picture to the front of greeting cards.

There are lots of ways that you can use your pictures, from greeting cards to buttons, box lids to key fobs – just perfect as gifts.

Customize your stuff by attaching different-sized pictures to your belongings. Create a matching set instantly!

Beautiful buttons

Like precious gems, covering these button bases with your work can make even the tiniest piece of embroidery look special. What a perfect way to use up scrap fabric and short ends of thread. Sew to your clothes to replace your buttons or wear as a brooch.

You will need

Scraps of fabric

Leftover embroidery threads

Sewing thread

Sewing needle

Embroidery needle

Button template for fabric size

Button base top and bottom

How to make a button

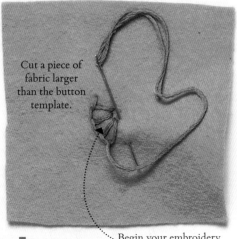

Cut a piece of fabric larger than the button template.

Begin your embroidery in the centre.

1

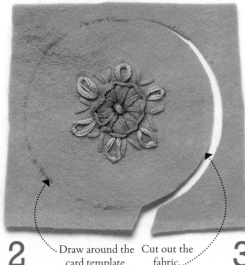

Draw around the card template.

Cut out the fabric.

2

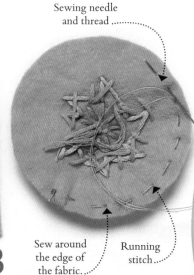

Sewing needle and thread

Sew around the edge of the fabric.

Running stitch

3

Place the button top in the centre of the fabric.

Gently pull the thread to gather the fabric.

4

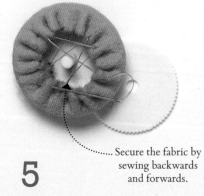

Secure the fabric by sewing backwards and forwards.

5

Press the back of the button down firmly.

6

Felt flower design
(See pages 22–24).

Stitch over the designs on
printed fabric (See page 27).

Cross-stitch motifs
(see pages 32–33).

Buttons galore
Experiment with the embroidery you have tried with the
other projects on the previous pages. These small areas are
great for practising your skills.

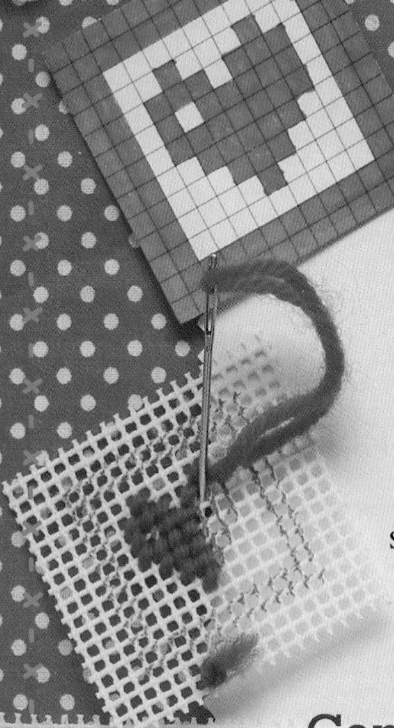

Needlepoint

Also known as tapestry, or canvas work, needlepoint is the craft of stitching onto a firm open-weave canvas. The stitches are worked on a canvas grid and tightly stitched so that none of the background is left showing.

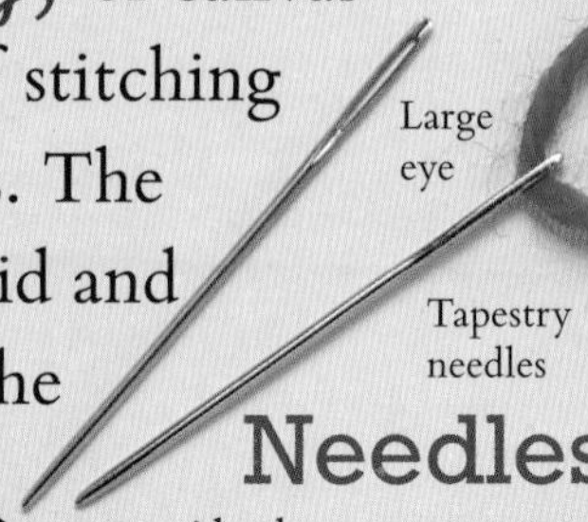

Large eye

Tapestry needles

Rounded end

Needles

Also known as tapestry needles, needlepoint needles have rounded ends. This helps to prevent the point from catching the canvas threads. The large eye makes it easy to thread.

Canvas

Canvas is made of cotton thread that has been treated to make it very stiff. It is sized by mesh sizes, or thread count per 2.5cm (1in); for example "10 count" means there are 10 threads to 2.5cm (1in). The sizes range from 5 count to 24 count; the smaller the mesh, the finer the stitches will be. Canvas can be bought with a pre-printed design in kits from craft shops, or plain in metre lengths.

The projects in this book use 10-count canvas – 10 threads to 2.5cm (1in)

Skeins of tapestry wool

Projects

There are all kinds of needlepoint equipment and materials available, from plastic canvas to kits with printed designs. The items shown here are all you need to complete the projects that follow and to create your own designs too.

Threads

Needlepoint thread comes in wool, cotton, or silk. Tapestry wool gives the best results on 10-count canvas, as the woollen stitches lay close together, completely hiding the canvas underneath. You can buy it in measured lengths called skeins.

Cutting the canvas

Taping the edges is optional.

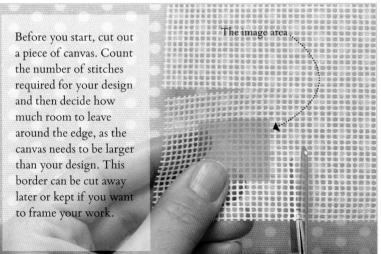

The image area

Before you start, cut out a piece of canvas. Count the number of stitches required for your design and then decide how much room to leave around the edge, as the canvas needs to be larger than your design. This border can be cut away later or kept if you want to frame your work.

If the wool keeps catching on the edge of the canvas, use masking tape to cover the edges.

Masking tape

Transferring designs

(See the project pages for designs as well as the templates on pages 122–123.)

Design your own image on squared paper.

Squared paper

Needlepoint designs are made up of squares, with each square representing a stitch. Notice that the stitch doesn't go in the holes of the canvas but across the threads. The design is just a guide. Create your own design or use one of the templates in this book.

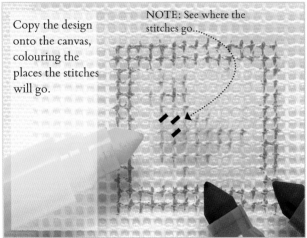

Copy the design onto the canvas, colouring the places the stitches will go.

NOTE: See where the stitches go...

Threading a tapestry needle

Cut a piece of wool 50cm (20in) long, thread the needle, and knot the end of the wool.

Fold the end of the wool over the needle and pull tight.

Pinch the loop between your fingers.

Put the eye of the needle over the loop.

Slide the eye of the needle down the loop.

Pull the wool through until the short end is out of the eye.

Begin stitching
These steps have been made using tent stitch.

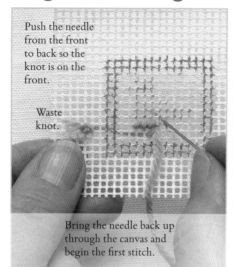

Push the needle from the front to back so the knot is on the front.

Waste knot.

Bring the needle back up through the canvas and begin the first stitch.

Continue stitching the same colour forwards and backwards.

Keep the stitch facing in the same direction.

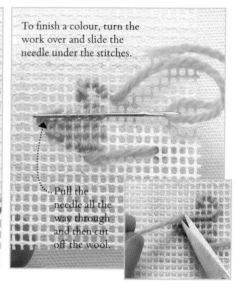

To finish a colour, turn the work over and slide the needle under the stitches.

Pull the needle all the way through and then cut off the wool.

Add new colour

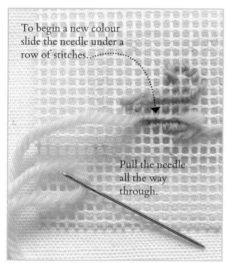

To begin a new colour slide the needle under a row of stitches.

Pull the needle all the way through.

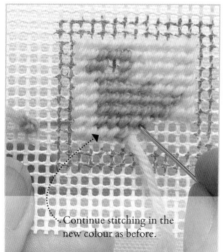

Continue stitching in the new colour as before.

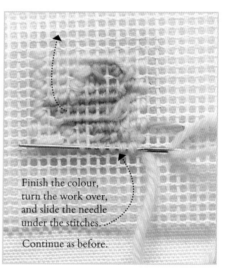

Finish the colour, turn the work over, and slide the needle under the stitches.

Continue as before.

Finishing off

Continue stitching the design following the pattern.

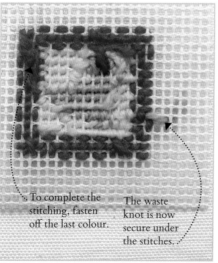

To complete the stitching, fasten off the last colour.

The waste knot is now secure under the stitches.

The waste knot can now be cut off.

Needlepoint stitches

Simple stitches Although there are lots of different styles of needlepoint stitches to choose from, here are four types of stitch to try in the projects that follow. The simplest is tent stitch, which is a small diagonal stitch. These examples of needlepoint show that by varying the size of the stitch, the direction it goes, and the colour combinations, many patterns and designs can be achieved.

Interlocking straight stitch

Tent stitch

Diagonal stitch

Cushion stitch

DIAGONAL STITCH

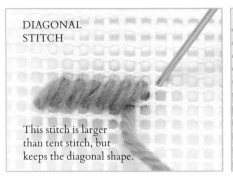

This stitch is larger than tent stitch, but keeps the diagonal shape.

Bring the needle up, then back in at a diagonal.

Bring the needle back through the canvas to the front, next to the first stitch.

Repeat steps until the end of a row.

DIAGONAL SQUARE

A diagonal stitch that varies in size to form a square shape.

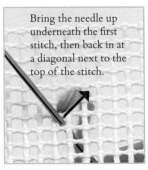
Bring the needle up underneath the first stitch, then back in at a diagonal next to the top of the stitch.

Pull the wool through to the back, then bring back to the front underneath the second stitch.

Complete the square shape by repeating the steps and following the lines below.

INTERLOCKING STRAIGHT STITCH

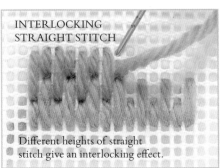

Different heights of straight stitch give an interlocking effect.

Bring the needle out of the canvas...

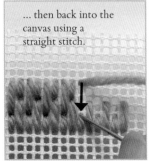
... then back into the canvas using a straight stitch.

Repeat these steps alternating long and short straight stitches.

Stripy pouch

Here's a chance to try out a variety of stitches and play with colours. Create simple stripy designs to decorate these handy little pouches – they're great for storing music players.

You will need
• 10-count canvas
• Tapestry wool in various colours • Tapestry needle •
Felt fabric • Sewing needle and thread

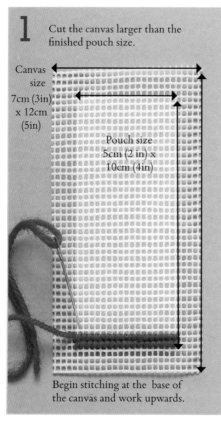

1 Cut the canvas larger than the finished pouch size.

Canvas size 7cm (3in) x 12cm (5in)

Pouch size 5cm (2 in) x 10cm (4in)

Begin stitching at the base of the canvas and work upwards.

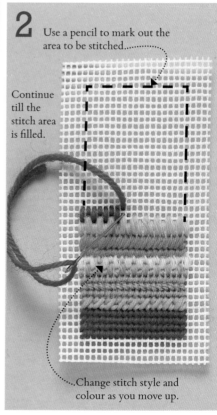

2 Use a pencil to mark out the area to be stitched.

Continue till the stitch area is filled.

Change stitch style and colour as you move up.

3 Carefully cut around the canvas.

Don't cut too close or the canvas will come apart.

4 Stitch over the edge of the canvas.

Continue all the way round the edge.

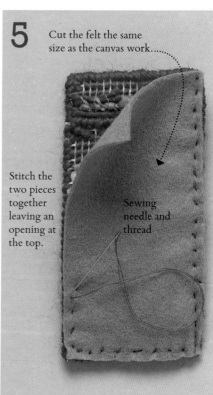

5 Cut the felt the same size as the canvas work.

Stitch the two pieces together leaving an opening at the top.

Sewing needle and thread

Gadget pouch

Perfect for keeping your phone or music player safely tucked away – you can use it for glasses too.

7cm (3in) x 12cm (5in)

Measure up

Decide what the pouch will be used for, like your music player for example. Measure its height and width – don't forget how thick it is too and include this in the width otherwise the pouch will be too tight.

Sewing pouch

Perfect for sewing essentials, such as small, sharp embroidery scissors.

5cm (2in) x 10cm (4in)

7cm (3in) x 12cm (5in)

All squared

See how many patterns you can make by simply using squares. Try the designs shown here or work out your own by drawing them on paper first. These cushions are ideal for pins but they can be any size you like.

You will need

Canvas

Tapestry needle

Tapestry wool

Felt for backing

Plus stuffing for the cushion.

Sewing needle

Cotton thread

How to make a cushion

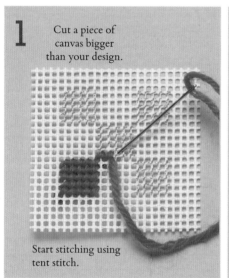

1 Cut a piece of canvas bigger than your design.

Start stitching using tent stitch.

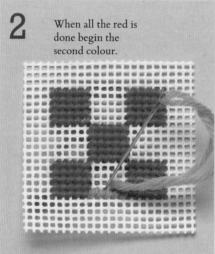

2 When all the red is done begin the second colour.

3 Cut off the canvas, but DON'T cut too close to the stitching.

4 Sew over the edge of the canvas.

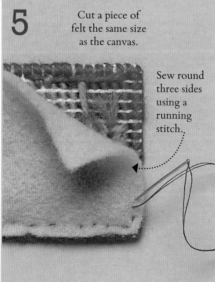

5 Cut a piece of felt the same size as the canvas.

Sew round three sides using a running stitch.

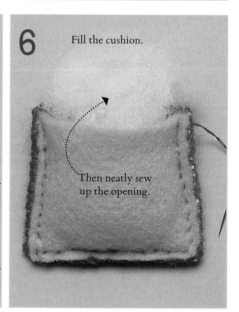

6 Fill the cushion.

Then neatly sew up the opening.

The biggest cushion here is 11cm (4½in) x 11cm (4½in); the smallest is 4cm (1½in) x 4cm (1½in).

Pin cushions

Pixel patches

Just like digital pictures these designs are made up of tiny squares. Each square is the same as one needlepoint stitch.

Use the graph paper to design your own pictures.

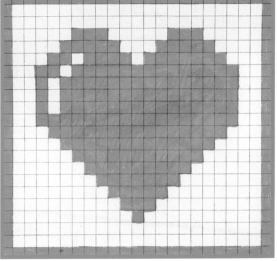

You will need

- Small pieces of canvas
- Tapestry wool and needle
- Graph paper and pen

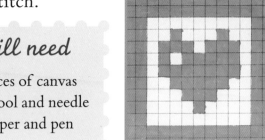

For more stitching patterns see pages 122–123.

How to make a patch

1

Cut the canvas bigger than the picture.

Start stitching the heart first.

2

Carefully cut out the patch leaving a border one hole width.

DON'T cut too close.

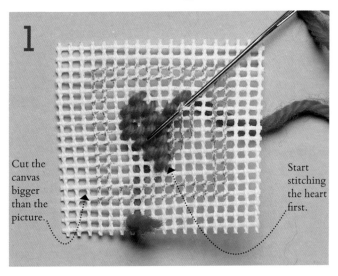

3

Stitch over the edge to finish off the patch.

4

You can now sew your patch onto your stuff or you can make a badge!

...To make a badge, sew a safety pin to a square of felt and glue the felt to your patch.

Handy tip

Your patches can be
sewn onto your bags.
You can also colour
coordinate your patches
to match your
clothes!

Rainbow frames

Canvas is a strong, stiff material which makes it ideal for these picture frames. Here is a simple design using bright, rainbow-coloured wool and just one style of stitch.

You will need
• Canvas • Tapestry wool in rainbow colours • Tapestry needle • Felt for backing • Sewing needle and thread • Thin card

How to make a small frame

1 Cut a piece of canvas 12cm (5in) x 12cm (5in).

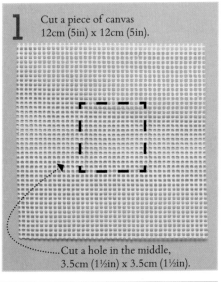

....Cut a hole in the middle, 3.5cm (1½in) x 3.5cm (1½in).

2 Start stitching from the centre. Change colour for each row.

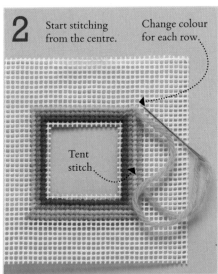

Tent stitch....

3 Cut the frame out of the canvas.

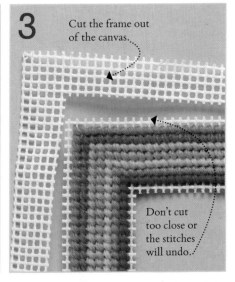

Don't cut too close or the stitches will undo....

4

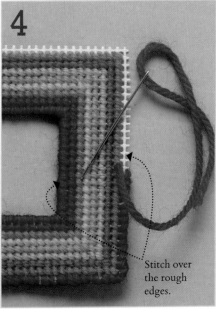

Stitch over the rough edges.

5 Cut a piece of felt the same size as the frame....

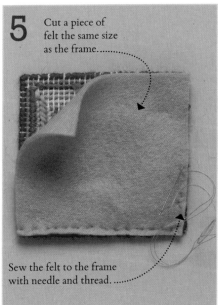

Sew the felt to the frame with needle and thread. ....

6

Cut the card small enough to slide into the frame.

Stick your picture to the card.

Frame it

Cut larger pieces of canvas depending on the size of your picture and how much frame you want to stitch. Experiment with different stitches and motifs.

Hang 'em up

Hang your handiwork on the wall with these little tabs. Cut a piece of ribbon and sew in place on the felt layer of the frame.

Cut ribbon 4cm (1½in) long.

Use a sewing needle and thread to attach the tab to the felt.

follow the pattern

Centre the design on the canvas and use the coloured squares to position the stitches and match the colours. Begin stitching the main part of the image first, then work the other colours one at a time.

You will need

A piece of canvas 10cm (4in) x 13cm (5in)

Selection of tapestry wool and needle

Felt pens

Pet portraits

Draw a picture of your favourite pet. With some pens and squared paper turn the portrait into coloured squares. No pets? No problem; stitch these little cats instead. Just use different-coloured wool if you want to change the cat colour or background.

Your pet design

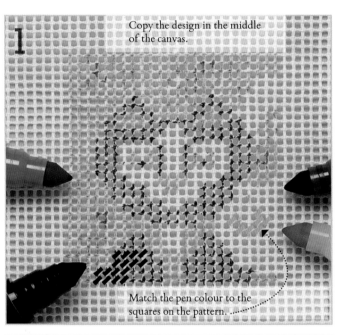

1 Copy the design in the middle of the canvas.

Match the pen colour to the squares on the pattern.

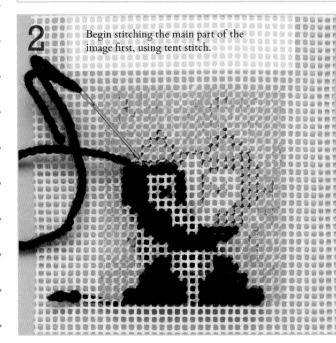

2 Begin stitching the main part of the image first, using tent stitch.

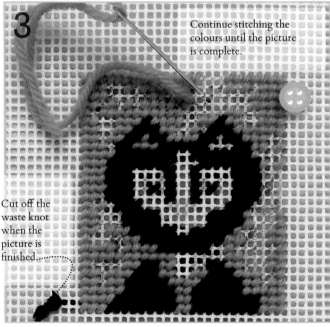

3 Continue stitching the colours until the picture is complete.

Cut off the waste knot when the picture is finished.

Patchwork

To make patchwork, small shaped pieces of fabric are sewn together in geometric patterns to create a large patterned cloth – a perfect way to reuse scraps and recycle clothes.

Paper for patches

Each fabric patch will need to be attached to a paper shape. You can reuse old envelopes and magazines to make these. You will need a lot as each patch has its own piece of paper, but they can be reused when the project is finished.

Patchwork fabric

Light-weight cotton is best for patchwork; don't use anything stretchy or too thick as it'll be difficult to make the patches even. Experiment with colours and patterns too.

Isometric paper to create designs (see templates on page 120)

Tracing paper

Old envelopes are good for paper patches.

Card for templates

Graph paper for patch designs

Sewing needle and pins

Sewing thread for tacking fabric to paper patches and sewing patches together

Card templates

Card from cereal boxes is ideal, but any card that is easy to cut out will do.

Ruler for drawing and measuring templates

Pencil to draw round the shapes

How patchwork works

Every patch needs a piece of fabric and a paper shape. The paper is tacked to the fabric, and then these patches are stitched together. The paper remains in the patch until you have finished. Templates made out of card are used to get the right size for the fabric and paper.

Square   Pentagon   Hexagon   Triangle

Patchwork pieces are based on these shapes.

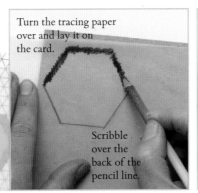

Copy the shape for the template onto tracing paper using a pencil (see page 120 for templates).

Turn the tracing paper over and lay it on the card.

Scribble over the back of the pencil line.

The pencil line will have transferred onto the card.

Card templates

Cut out the card shapes.

The large shape is for the fabric.

The smaller shape is for the paper.

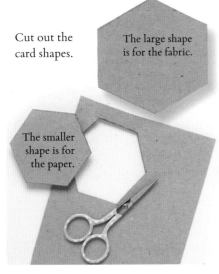

Preparing the paper shapes

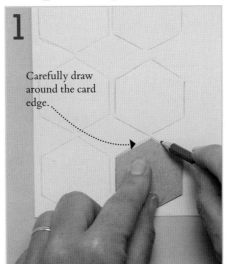

1

Carefully draw around the card edge.

2

Cut out the paper shapes.

It's important to draw and cut the shapes accurately, because they will determine the shape of your final patch.

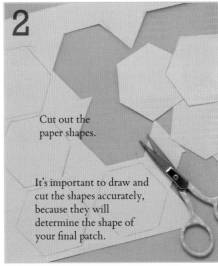

Preparing the fabric

1

Select some fabrics that work well together.

Use the large card template for the fabric.

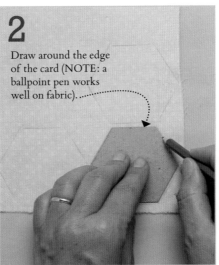

2

Draw around the edge of the card (NOTE: a ballpoint pen works well on fabric).

3

Cut out the fabric shapes.

Preparing the patches

1 Fold the fabric over the paper.

Carefully pin the paper in the centre of the fabric.

REVERSE SIDE OF FABRIC

Hold the fabric in place as you stitch.

2 Use tacking stitch to attach the fabric.

Stitch over the corner to hold it in place.

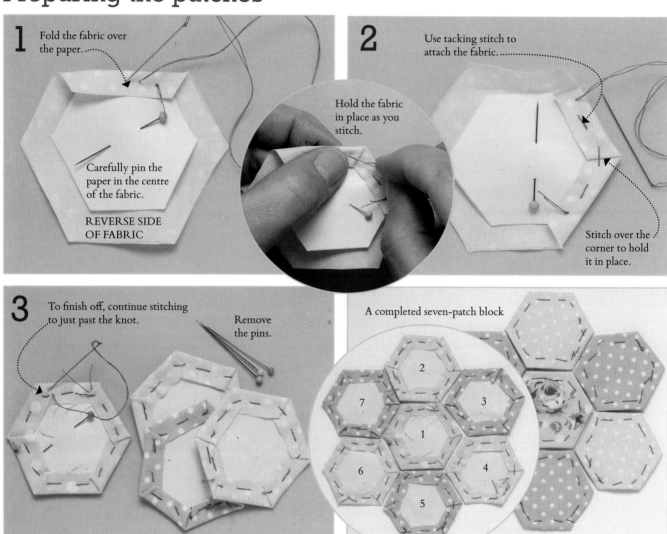

3 To finish off, continue stitching to just past the knot.

Remove the pins.

A completed seven-patch block

Sewing patches together

1 Place the patches together with their fronts facing each other.

Use tiny stitches to oversew the edges.

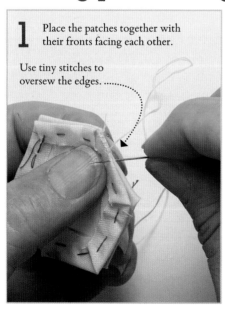

2 At the end of the patch, stitch back over your last few stitches to secure.

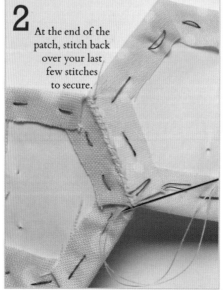

3 Continue stitching the rest of the patches together.

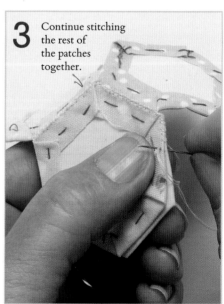

Removing the paper patch

! When all the patches are sewn together, press them flat with an iron.

Cut the tacking thread and pull it out.

Carefully remove the paper templates.

Pressing the patch

Once the paper has been removed, the patches are quite flimsy and the folded seams will tend to unfold. To keep them in shape, press with a hot iron.

! BE CAREFUL – IRONS ARE HOT!

ASK FOR HELP WHEN USING ONE.

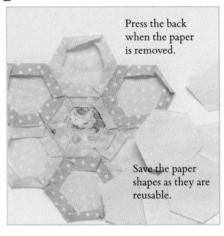

Press the back when the paper is removed.

Save the paper shapes as they are reusable.

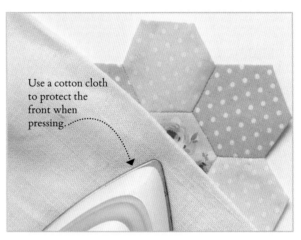

Use a cotton cloth to protect the front when pressing.

Patchwork pattern blocks

Triangles can be used to make up blocks of larger triangles or squares.

Blocks When patches are sewn together like this they are known as blocks. These blocks can help when making large pieces. Placing the blocks in different ways creates all sorts of new designs.

Six-sided shapes, sewn together, make a seven-patch block.

Squares can be joined to make a 9-patch block.

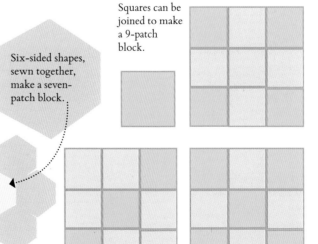

Patchwork squares

Make a comfy bed cover for a sleepy toy. This patchwork of squares using two different fabrics is one of the easiest designs to put together. Make the squares bigger and create cushions and bags.

You will need

- Two pieces of contrasting fabric • 9 paper squares • Felt for backing • Sewing thread to match fabric • Dark coloured sewing thread for tacking • Sewing needle

How to put the patches together

Cut out 9 PAPER PIECES 5cm (2in) x 5cm (2in).

Cut out 9 FABRIC PIECES 7cm (3in) x 7cm (3in).

1 Place the paper in the centre of the fabric.

Fold the fabric over the edge of the paper.

2 Sew the fabric to the paper using large stitches.

3 Stitch all the way around.

4 Sew the squares together.

Matching thread

Make the stitches small and neat.

5 Undo the tacking stitch and remove the paper.

Cut the felt to the same size as the sewn patches.

Make the most of the fabric designs by putting them in the centre of the patch.

Carefully stitch the felt to the patches using running stitch.

Z Zz z

Z z z

Handy tip

This design can be used to make cushion covers by making the squares larger. Try 9cm (3½in) x 9cm (3½in) squares.

Squares and triangles

Lots of patterns can be made by placing blocks of triangles in different ways. Choose fabrics with very different contrasting colours and patterns for more dramatic effects.

Make a block

Make four triangular patches on using the template on page 120. Try using the squared graph paper.

Pin the paper template in the centre of the fabric.

Fold the fabric over the paper and sew in place.

You will need

- 4 different fabric designs • Paper templates (see page 120) • Sewing thread and needle

Make four triangles the same size.

Stitch the triangles together.

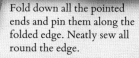

Fold down all the pointed ends and pin them along the folded edge. Neatly sew all round the edge.

Join blocks together

Turn each block around so the triangles match up differently.

Make three more blocks in the same way.

Sew the four blocks together on the reverse side using small stitches.

Remove the paper and use an iron to press the reverse side flat.

Project idea

This design has been used to decorate a cushion. Place the block design centrally on the cushion and neatly sew it on. If you sew lots of blocks together you can make a big floor cushion.

Patchy cushions

Shaped like a honeycomb, these six-sided patches are sewn together to make a seven-patch block. Here two blocks have been stitched together and stuffed to make cushions.

You will need

• 14 prepared six-sided patches (use the template on page 120) • Sewing thread and needle • Stuffing

Make 2 x seven-patch blocks

To make the blocks follow the steps on pages 50–53.

This design uses a different fabric for each patch.

To help flatten the fabric, iron the blocks before removing the paper.

How to make a pin cushion

1 Remove the template paper.

...Iron the fabric edges flat again at this stage.

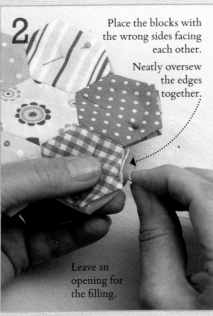

2 Place the blocks with the wrong sides facing each other.

Neatly oversew the edges together.

Leave an opening for the filling.

3 Fill the cushion, working the stuffing into the corners. ...

Neatly sew up the opening.

Little and Large

It's so simple; the size of the patch will make a smaller or larger cushion. Go to page 120 and try out some different sized templates.

Match the patch

The seven-patch blocks can be sewn together to become a larger piece of fabric, such as a quilt for your bed.

Five-sided patches

Take 12 patches, stitch them all together and, as if by magic, they turn into these charming soft balls. They make perfect presents for babies and for cat lovers try putting some catnip in with the stuffing – it'll make their pets very happy.

Handy tip
The template shown is to make the smaller ball. To make the larger ball increase the size of the template.

Did you know?
A twelve-sided object is called a **dodecahedron** – who would have guessed these patchwork balls could have such a serious name! A five-sided shape is called a **pentagon.**

You will need
• Variety of light weight fabric such as cotton
• Card and paper template • Sewing needle
• Sewing thread, matching and contrasting colour • Soft-toy stuffing

Five-sided template

Two sizes The large shape to be cut in card, the small shape to be cut out of paper.

Trace over the shape, cutting a piece of thin card to the large size and using paper for the small size.

SMALL PAPER SHAPE

Fold the fabric over this small shape.

LARGE CARD SHAPE

Cut the fabric to this size.

A flower shape

Six patches sewn together

...Tacking stitches hold the backing paper in place.

Patchy decoration

If you're happy with just the flower shape why not leave it at that and use it as a motif. Remove the paper templates first – here it has sewn onto the front of a bag.

Patch match

For a really fancy ball choose at least six different fabrics – pick them carefully; they don't have to match, just look good together.

Dark sewing thread for the tacking stitches

Sewing thread to match the fabric

Sewing needle

How to make patchwork balls

You will need 12 five-sided patches. Stitch the patches together as shown below and make two cup shapes. Match up the cups and stitch them together leaving an opening for the stuffing.

Arrange the patches so each patch is next to a different fabric.

Draw around the card template.

Cut out 12 fabric pieces.

Place the paper template in the centre.

Use a different coloured thread.

Tack the fabric over the edge of the paper.

Make a flower shape x 2

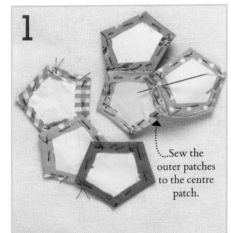

1

...Sew the outer patches to the centre patch.

2

Repeat step 1 to create another flower shape like this.

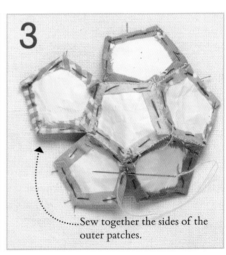

3

....Sew together the sides of the outer patches.

4

When all the sides are sewn up they will form a cup shape.

To achieve the ball shape join the two cups together by matching the tip of the patches on one of the cups into the "V" shape space on the other.

5 Make two cup shapes

Place this point into the V shape of the other cup.

Stitch two cups together

1 Stitch the patches together.

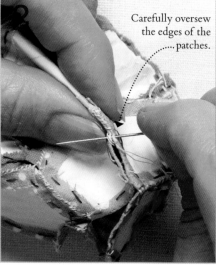

Carefully oversew the edges of the patches.

3 Leave an opening to allow for the filling.

Forming a ball

1 Remove the tacking stitches.

Discard the paper templates.

2 Turn the ball inside out.

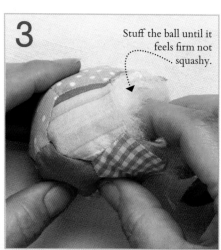

3 Stuff the ball until it feels firm not squashy.

Finish the ball

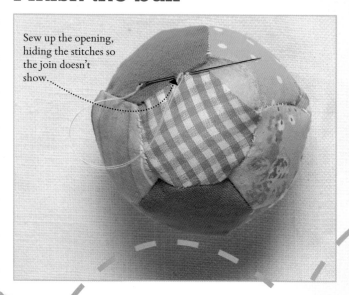

Sew up the opening, hiding the stitches so the join doesn't show.

Pretty puffs

These dainty puffed shapes are simply made from circles of cotton fabric gathered up tight – puffect!

Puff necklace

Create a garland of puffs by sewing them together. Add buttons to the middles and ribbon for ties.

Join the puffs together.

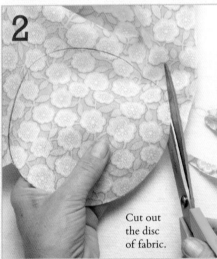

Decorate the puffs with buttons.

Make a Puff

You will need

- A circular template 15cm (6in) across
- Scraps of cotton fabric
- Sewing thread and needle
- Ballpoint pen

1 Using a bowl as a template, draw around the edge.

2 Cut out the disc of fabric.

3 Fold over 7mm (¼in) of the fabric edge and hem.

Use loose running stitch to sew around the edge.

4 Once the hem is stitched, gently pull the thread to gather up the fabric.

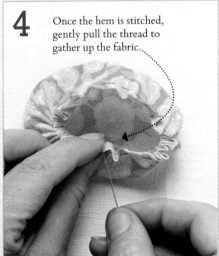

5 Work the fabric around to make the gathers even.

Sew a couple of stitches to secure the gathers.

Join them up

Puffs are a traditional patchwork technique. Try joining lots of puffs together to make a cover for a plain cushion or join even more together and make a colourful bed throw.

Carefully sew through the edges of the puffs.

Appliqué

What is appliqué? Well, it's pictures and patterns made by sewing small fabric shapes to a piece of material. Motifs can be used like patches to dress up clothing. Sewing stitches can be invisible but embroidery stitches are a perfect way to add decoration.

Tracing paper

Transfer paper

Tracing paper

Use this for copying an image and transferring the outline as a pattern for your piece of fabric.

Transfer paper

Used in dress making and craft projects, this paper has a glued backing that, when heated, can be used to attach motifs to the fabric items.

Fabrics

Light-weight cotton fabric is best for appliqué. As well as coming in an array of colours and patterns, it is easy to cut and shape. The cut edges will fray but stitching the edges and using adhesive transfer paper will help. Avoid stretchy fabric as this can distort the motif shapes.

Buttons for decoration

Needles and pins

Embroidery thread

Sewing thread

Scissors for cutting out shapes

Pencil for tracing motifs

Felt fabric

Felt will not fray like other fabrics because of the way it is made. This makes it ideal for appliqué as even the smallest motifs will keep their shape.

Transferring designs using transfer paper

What is transfer paper?

Transfer paper is a handy way to attach motifs to the fabric items you want to decorate. It's like tracing paper with glue on one side. It works in two steps; first you stick the paper shape to your motif fabric and then you iron the motif to the fabric you are decorating. Use the maker's instructions.

1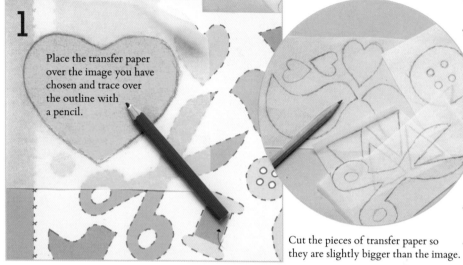

Place the transfer paper over the image you have chosen and trace over the outline with a pencil.

Cut the pieces of transfer paper so they are slightly bigger than the image.

2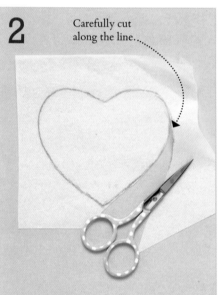

Carefully cut along the line.

3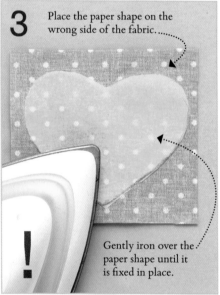

Place the paper shape on the wrong side of the fabric.

Gently iron over the paper shape until it is fixed in place.

4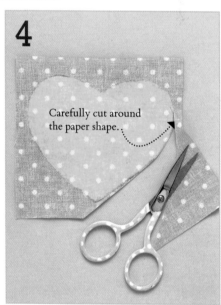

Carefully cut around the paper shape.

5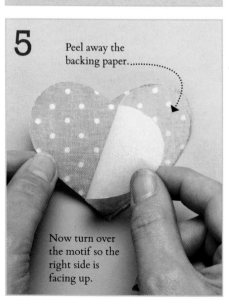

Peel away the backing paper.

Now turn over the motif so the right side is facing up.

6

Carefully position the motif where you want it to go.

Gently iron all over the motif until it is stuck down.

Using an iron

CAREFUL – IRONS ARE HOT! ASK FOR HELP IF USING ONE.

• The iron will need to be hot to make the transfer paper work effectively.

• PLEASE NOTE: Some fabrics will melt if you iron them. Place a piece of cotton cloth over the fabric motif before ironing to prevent this happening.

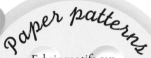

Paper patterns

Fabric motifs can be attached by simply pinning them directly to the base fabric. Trace over the image and cut out the shape, then using the tracing-paper shape, cut out the fabric motif.

Decorative stitching

Stitches used for attaching the motifs can be tiny and invisible, using sewing thread, or they can be made to be part of the design. Try using the stitches from the Embroidery pages of the book (pages 14–35). Here are three decorative ways of making stitches part of the design using embroidery thread.

Tracing paper template

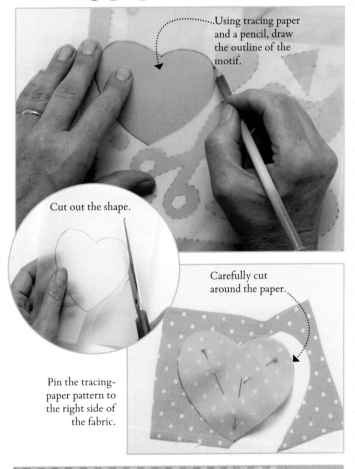

Using tracing paper and a pencil, draw the outline of the motif.

Cut out the shape.

Carefully cut around the paper.

Pin the tracing-paper pattern to the right side of the fabric.

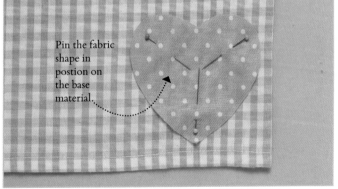

Pin the fabric shape in postion on the base material.

RUNNING STITCH

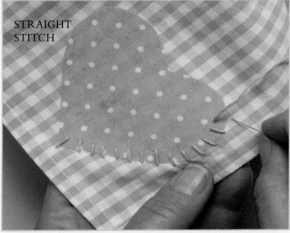

STRAIGHT STITCH

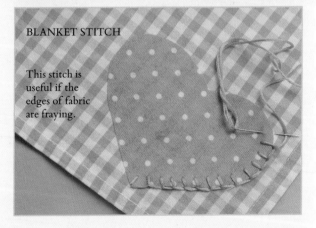

BLANKET STITCH

This stitch is useful if the edges of fabric are fraying.

Ready-made motifs

Look out for fabric with big, bold designs because these make perfect motifs.

DIY shapes

Design your own motifs. If you can't find a design you like or you have a picture in mind, draw the design on paper and use this as your pattern. Cut out the shapes and pin them to the fabric, then cut out to make the fabric shapes.

Handy tip

If you don't have any adhesive transfer paper, simply cut out the shapes, pin them to the backing material, and sew them in place.

! Iron the paper on the reverse of the fabric, over the motif.

Cut out the motif.

! Iron the motif in position.

Cup-cake bag

Create a delicious cup-cake bag made of felt and buttons. First draw your design on paper, then cut it out to use as the pattern. Felt is great because it doesn't fray at the edges.

You will need

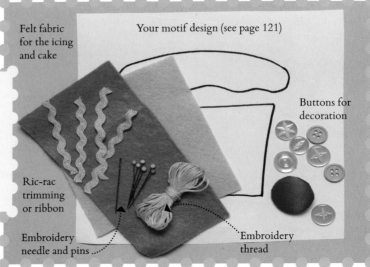

Felt fabric for the icing and cake

Your motif design (see page 121)

Buttons for decoration

Ric-rac trimming or ribbon

Embroidery needle and pins

Embroidery thread

Bag size

Cut out a piece of fabric 20cm (8in) x 42cm (16in). Position the motif in the top half of the fabric, as shown below. Remember to allow space for the seams and for turning over at the top of the bag.

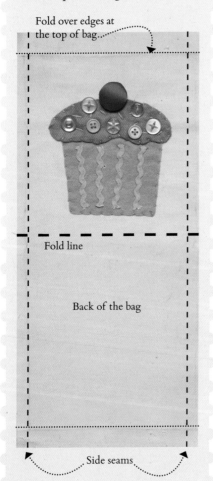

Fold over edges at the top of bag

Fold line

Back of the bag

Side seams

How to make the motif

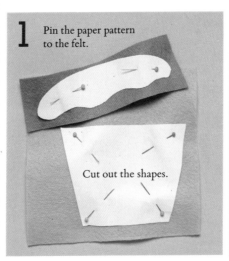

1 Pin the paper pattern to the felt.

Cut out the shapes.

2 Pin the felt to the backing fabric.

Use bold stitches to attach the felt.

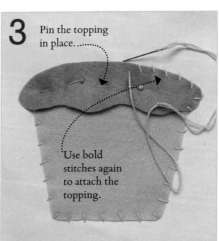

3 Pin the topping in place.

Use bold stitches again to attach the topping.

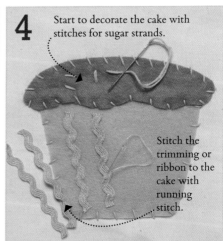

4 Start to decorate the cake with stitches for sugar strands.

Stitch the trimming or ribbon to the cake with running stitch.

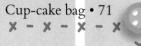

Ready-made

If you already have a bag, why not decorate that instead? Just follow the motif step-by-steps in the same way.

Use ribbon or trimming to look like the sides of a cake case.

Collect up buttons to decorate your work.

Make a bag

Fold the fabric in half, right sides facing. Fold the tops of the bag over and stitch in place on either side. Sew together the sides using back stitch. Finally, pin the handles on and sew them in position (see pages 118–119 for more bags).

Fold over the fabric at the top and sew up the sides.

Pin the handles to the bag and sew them in place.

Mmm ... doughnuts

Which flavour to make, chocolate or plain? It's easy to do – just change the felt colour. Appliqué the icing, then finish your doughnuts off with a sprinkle of stitches. They look good enough to eat!

Cut out a template

Cut out two circles of felt for the doughnut.

Cut out one piece of coloured felt for the icing.

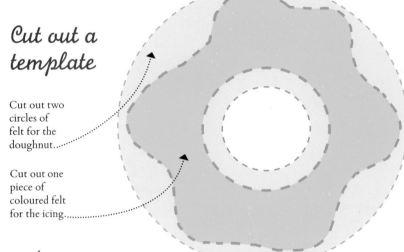

How to make a doughnut

You will need

Felt shapes for doughnut and icing.

Needles and thread for sewing and embroidery

1 You'll need some stuffing fibre too.

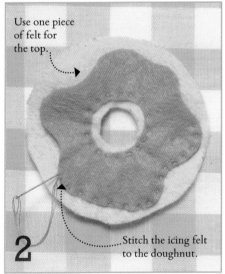

Use one piece of felt for the top.

Stitch the icing felt to the doughnut.

2

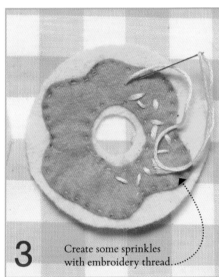

Create some sprinkles with embroidery thread.

3

Second piece of felt.

Stitch the two pieces of doughnut felt together.

4 Leave an opening for the stuffing.

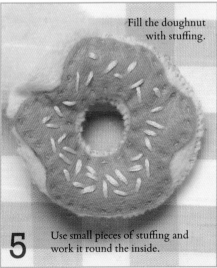

Fill the doughnut with stuffing.

5 Use small pieces of stuffing and work it round the inside.

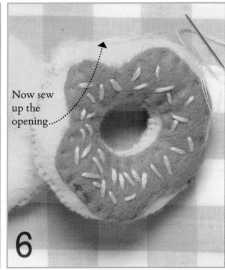

Now sew up the opening.

6

Handy tip

To help get the stuffing to go all the way round the doughnut try gently pushing it into place with a blunt pencil – though don't push too hard or you'll go through the stitching.

Sprinkles of stitches

Try a mix of colours to give the effect of sugar strands and sprinkles. Try adding beads for a 3D effect.

Birds, bunting, and buttons

Make beautiful crafty boxes.

By using even the smallest scraps of fabric, appliqué is a perfect way to create patches to decorate boxes and bags. These sewing-theme motifs are a lovely finish to your craft kit.

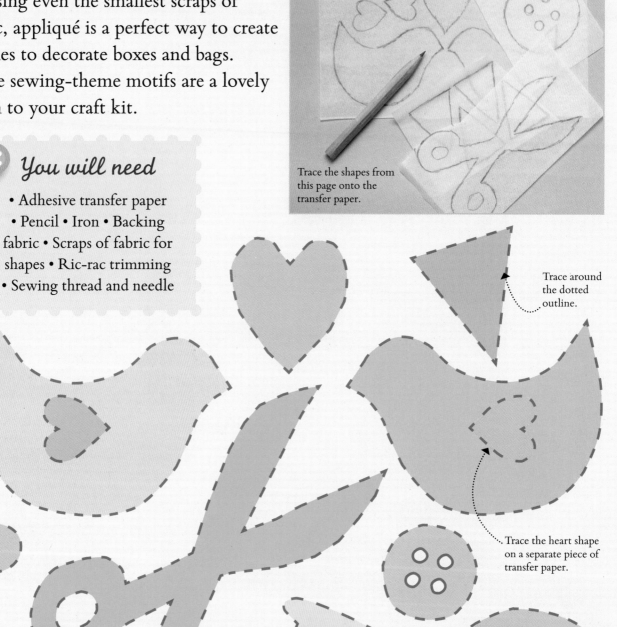

Trace the shapes from this page onto the transfer paper.

You will need

- Adhesive transfer paper
- Pencil • Iron • Backing fabric • Scraps of fabric for shapes • Ric-rac trimming
- Sewing thread and needle

Trace around the dotted outline.

Trace the heart shape on a separate piece of transfer paper.

Use this shape for the needle case on pages 78–79.

Position the shapes

WARNING: THE IRON IS HOT!

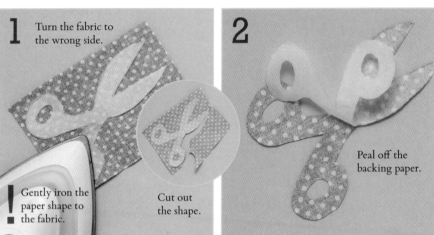

1 Turn the fabric to the wrong side.

Gently iron the paper shape to the fabric.

Cut out the shape.

2 Peal off the backing paper.

3 Place the shape right side up on the fabric.

Gently iron the shape onto the fabric.

Scissor design

Collect together all the pieces to decorate the fabric patch. The ric-rac border and very small bits of fabric do not need the adhesive backing.

Ric-rac border

Sew the shape to the fabric patch with running stitch.

The stitches are for decoration so keep them neat and even.

Small shapes and buttons can be sewn directly to the patch.

Position the ric-rac border with pins then sew in place.

Match the ends of the ric-rac to look neat.

Carefully snip holes for the fabric buttons.

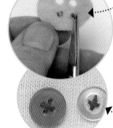

Sew on the buttons with different-coloured thread.

Birds and bunting

Cut out a piece of fabric for the patch.

Cut out the fabric shapes.

Prepare the shapes to be ironed on (as above).

Make a feature of the running stitches.

Use French knots for the eyes.

Use blanket stitch for a decorative edge.

Use running stitch to create extra detail.

Pin cushion

This big button motif makes a pretty pincushion or button-box lid.

Big button design

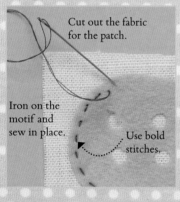

Cut out the fabric for the patch.

Iron on the motif and sew in place.

Use bold stitches.

Finish it off with a ric-rac border.

Craft in a bag

Here a patch has been sewn to a small tote bag – a handy place to keep your craft materials.

More ideas

The finished patches can be applied to all kinds of surfaces. Either stitch them to fabric like this bag or glue them onto a box lid.

Needle case

Keep all your needles and pins at hand in a simple cloth case. This design helps you practise your sewing skills – sewing buttons and appliqué.

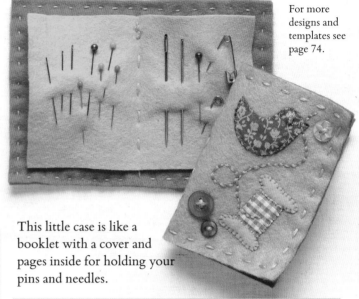

For more designs and templates see page 74.

This little case is like a booklet with a cover and pages inside for holding your pins and needles.

You will need

Cut out fabric bird shape and bobbin.

Sewing needle and embroidery needle

For the cover: Cut out two pieces of fabric 14.5cm (5½in) x 10.5cm (4in).

For the inside: Cut out one piece of fabric 12cm (5in) x 9cm (3½in).

Embroidery thread

Sewing thread

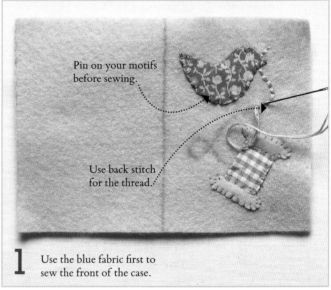

Pin on your motifs before sewing.

Use back stitch for the thread.

1 Use the blue fabric first to sew the front of the case.

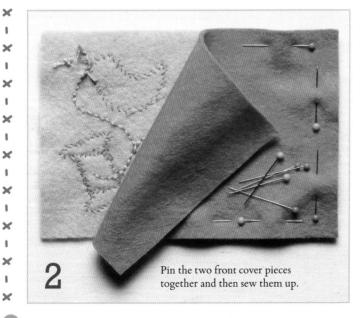

2 Pin the two front cover pieces together and then sew them up.

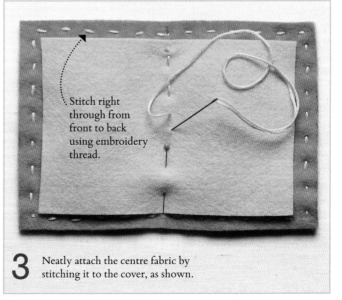

Stitch right through from front to back using embroidery thread.

3 Neatly attach the centre fabric by stitching it to the cover, as shown.

Ready-made

Patterned fabrics are perfect places to find ready-made motifs. Simply cut out an image and sew with embroidery stitches to decorate your wardrobe.

Draw a heart shape around the image and cut it out.

Attach the heart motif with blanket stitch.

Sweet heart

This cute little motif has been made by selecting an area on a piece a fabric, drawing a heart shape to frame the image, cutting it out then sewing it in place.

Flower shapes

Select a motif and iron on the adhesive transfer paper.

Select the flower you want and either use the iron-on transfer paper method to attach it to the backing fabric or sew it directly in position. Use embroidery stitches (see pages 16–18) to decorate the flower. Use contrasting colours and add buttons for extra decoration.

Stitch crazy

Cut out the shapes and attach them to your clothes then go wild with the stitching. Transform a simple flower design into something stunning.

Tiny pictures make perfect little patches. Frame in blanket stitch with colourful embroidery thread.

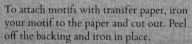

To attach motifs with transfer paper, iron your motif to the paper and cut out. Peel off the backing and iron in place.

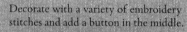

Decorate with a variety of embroidery stitches and add a button in the middle.

Knitting

Two needles and a ball of yarn are all you need to get knitting. Work the stitches from one needle to the other and see the fabric grow.

KNITTING RULES

There are no set rules about how to use the yarn and needle – knitters all round the world use them in quite different ways. The following pages show two methods, one of which is preferred by left-handers.

Knitting needles

Knitting needles are available in many different sizes, from very narrow ones for fine work to very thick ones that produce a chunky knit. The projects that follow use a medium sized needle.

Tapestry needle for sewing up projects

Knitting spool

Also known as a Knitting Nancy and French Knitting, this gadget knits yarn into long braids that can be used with all kinds of projects.

The pin is used to work the yarn over the top of hooks on the spool.

4mm knitting needles

Stitch types

There are two stitch types used in the projects that follow 'Knit stitch' and 'Purl stitch'. Knitting patterns shorten the names as shown below:

K = knit
P = purl
st = stitch

Braids made with the knitting spool.

"Double knit" (DK) yarn

Yarns

The many different types of yarn are described by their 'weight'. The yarn used for the projects that follow is a "Double Knit" or DK weight and made of either wool or acrylic. Other yarns are known as 4-ply and chunky. Each yarn will produce a different feel to the fabric.

How to get started

Knitting is produced with two needles, one held in each hand. To begin, you need to make stitches – this is called "casting on". You will need to cast on the number of stitches required in the pattern. The stitches that are being worked will be on the left hand needle and the ones you have made will go on the right.

These loops are called stitches.

Ball of yarn

Knitted rows

Knitting needle

Slip knot
The first stitch on the needle is knotted so the yarn stays on.

Loop the end of the yarn around your finger tips.

Push the yarn through the loop with your finger.

Pull the yarn through to make a loop.

Slide the new loop onto the needle.

Pull on the ball end of the yarn to tighten the loop.

Casting on
There are many ways to cast on. This method uses your thumb.

1 Wrap the yarn around your thumb as shown.

2 Pick up the yarn with the needle.

3 Let the yarn go from your thumb onto the needle.

4 Continue doing this until you have enough stitches.

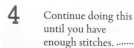

Counting rows
When using a pattern that requires lots of rows, it is sometimes tricky to keep count. Either keep a note on paper and tick them off or try this handy little gadget that fits on the end of your needle.

Turn the dial for each new row.

. . . 5, 4, 3, 2, 1 stitches

Now you are ready to KNIT!

Each new row will begin with the first stitch on the right.

Knit stitch

Also called plain stitch, this stitch is generally thought to be the easiest to make and is certainly a useful basic stitch for simple projects.

For knit stitch, the right-hand needle goes to the back of the stitch.

The yarn also goes at the back.

Method 1 (This is the English method.)

1 Hold the knitting with your hands in this position.

Take the yarn around the back.

Place the needle in the back of the stitch.

2 Wrap the yarn under and round the needle from right to left.

Method 2 (This is the Continental method; it might be helpful for left-handers.)

1 Place the yarn between the fingers of your left hand.

2 Use your index finger to move the yarn.

Your middle finger and thumb are used to hold the knitting in place.

Take the yarn around the front of the needle.

Garter Stitch

Garter stitch isn't an actual stitch but the name given to a piece of knitting where every row is knitted in knit stitch. The effect is bobbly on both sides.

Garter stitch is also made if you knit every row in purl stitch.

3 Pull on the yarn and move the needle from the back to the front.

4 The right needle is now on top of the left one and has taken the stitch with it.

5 Slide the top needle to the right. The stitch will now be transferred onto the right needle, completing the stitch.

Begin the next stitch as in step 1.

3 Bring the yarn down firmly between the needles.

4 Bring the needle with the loop of yarn to the front.

5 Take the needle with the stitch off the left hand needle.

Begin the next stitch as in step 1.

Making shapes

You can shape the knitting by adding (increasing) or taking away (decreasing) stitches. There are many different ways to do this, but here are two simple methods which you can use for the projects in this book.

INCREASE SHAPE

An extra stitch has been made at the beginning and the end of each row.

Two stitches have been knitted together at the beginning and end of each row.

DECREASE SHAPE

Make a stitch - increasing

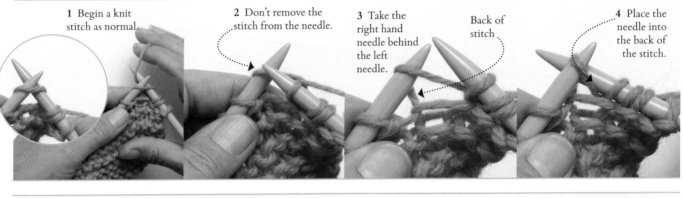

1 Begin a knit stitch as normal.

2 Don't remove the stitch from the needle.

3 Take the right hand needle behind the left needle.

Back of stitch

4 Place the needle into the back of the stitch.

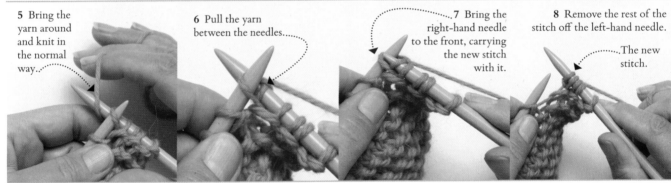

5 Bring the yarn around and knit in the normal way.

6 Pull the yarn between the needles.

7 Bring the right-hand needle to the front, carrying the new stitch with it.

8 Remove the rest of the stitch off the left-hand needle.

The new stitch.

Knit two together - decreasing

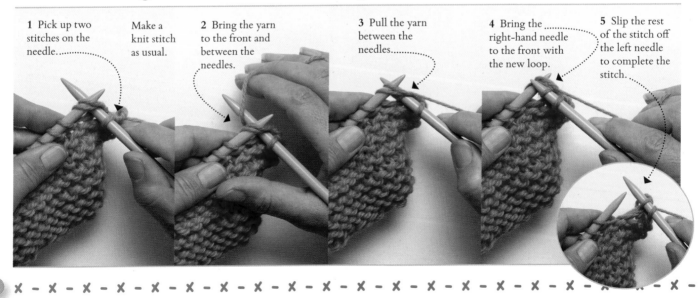

1 Pick up two stitches on the needle.

Make a knit stitch as usual.

2 Bring the yarn to the front and between the needles.

3 Pull the yarn between the needles.

4 Bring the right-hand needle to the front with the new loop.

5 Slip the rest of the stitch off the left needle to complete the stitch.

Join new yarn

1 Tie the new yarn to the old yarn with a loose knot.

2 Slide the knot up the yarn to the needle.

3 Continue knitting as usual.

Knit in new colour

Here the knitting is shown on the reverse side. Join the new yarn as shown (left). To tidy up the loose ends of both colours, gather them up with the working yarn as you knit.

Casting off

1 Begin the row by knitting two stitches.

2 Pick up the first stitch with the left needle.

3 Carry this first stitch over the second stitch and over the end of the needle.

4 Repeat steps 1–3...

5 ...until one stitch remains. Open up the loop

6 Cut the yarn and place the end in the loop.

7 Pull the yarn to close the loop.

Tidy away ends (Sewing in ends when adding new yarn or tidying the loose ends of finished pieces).

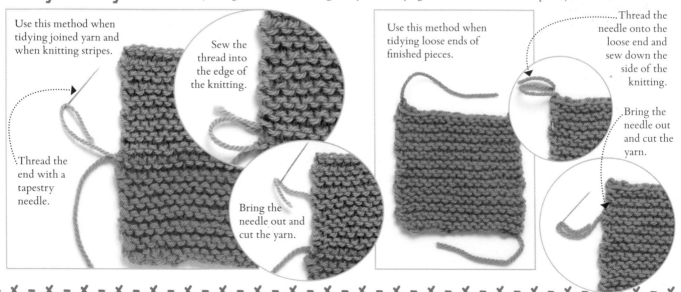

Use this method when tidying joined yarn and when knitting stripes.

Thread the end with a tapestry needle.

Sew the thread into the edge of the knitting.

Bring the needle out and cut the yarn.

Use this method when tidying loose ends of finished pieces.

Thread the needle onto the loose end and sew down the side of the knitting.

Bring the needle out and cut the yarn.

Just knit it!

Master knit stitch and you can make plenty of things just by using one stitch. Here's a chance for you to practise your skills.

You will need

- 4mm knitting needles
- Double knit yarn

HAT
2 x 50-gm
balls

SCARF
2 x 50-gm
balls

BAG
1 x 50-gm
ball

STRAP
1 x 50-gm
ball

RIBBON
1 x 50-gm
ball

Hat

Cast on 50 stitches.
Row 1 knit stitch.
Continue using knit stitch until it measures 40cm (16in).
Cast off.

Scarf

Cast on 24 stitches.
Row 1 knit stitch.
Continue using knit stitch until it measures 90cm (36in).
Cast off.

Bag

Cast on 14 stitches.
Row 1 knit stitch.
Continue using knit stitch until it measures 24cm (10in).
Cast off.

Bag strap

Cast on 3 stitches.
Row 1 knit stitch.
Continue using knit stitch until it measures 76cm (30in).
Cast off.

Ribbon

Cast on 6 stitches.
Row 1 knit stitch.
Continue using knit stitch until it measures 40cm (16in).
Cast off.

HAT

RIBBON

SCARF

BAG
STRAP

BAG

Button up

These plain knits can be
easily brightened up – try
adding colourful buttons
or mix up the colours by
adding a multicoloured
fringe to your scarf.

How to make hats, scarves, bags, and bows

Start by sewing the loose ends into the pieces of knitting (see page 87). Use a tapestry needle and the yarn that you used to make the item to sew the pieces together. When you have finished, use buttons to decorate the pieces.

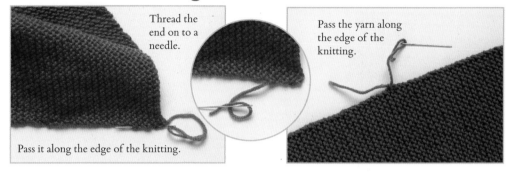

Thread the end on to a needle.

Pass it along the edge of the knitting.

Pass the yarn along the edge of the knitting.

Make a hat

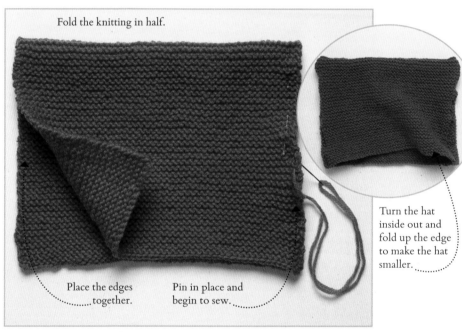

Fold the knitting in half.

Place the edges together.

Pin in place and begin to sew.

Turn the hat inside out and fold up the edge to make the hat smaller.

Make a bag

Fold the knitting in half.

Pin the sides together.

Stitch together with back stitch.

Attach the strap to the edge of the bag.

Making tassels

Sew in the loose ends and where the yarn is joined.

The thickness of the tassel can vary depending on how many loops of yarn you make. Cut a piece of card twice the length you'd like your tassels. Tie the yarn to the card and wind it around 8 times. Cut the yarn at the top and bottom of the card. To make a tassel take two strands and fold them in half.

Tie the yarn to the card.

Cut the yarn at the top and bottom.

Fold two strands in half.

1 Push a large crochet hook through the edge of the knitting.

Hook up the two folded strands of yarn.

2 Carefully take the hook back through the knitting, pulling the yarn with it.

3 Remove the hook.

4 Place the yarn ends through the loop to create a loose knot.

5 Space the tassels evenly across the end of the scarf.

Cut the tassels to the same length when they are all in place.

Make a bow

You can also simply tie your ribbon into a bow.

Fold one end over across the middle.

Fold the other end over across the first.

Sew in place with a couple of stitches.

Purl stitch

It's all front with purl stitch. The yarn is worked from the front and the needle goes in the front of the stitch.

For purl stitch, the needle goes in the front of the stitch.

The yarn also goes at the front too.

Method 1 (The English method)

1 Hold the knitting with your hands in this position.

Bring the yarn to the front.

Place the needle in the front of the stitch.

2 Take the yarn between the needles.

3 Wrap it round the needle from right to left.

Method 2 (The Continental method; left-handers might find this method helpful.)

1 Place the right hand needle in the front of the stitch.

Wind the yarn around your fingers.

2 Bring the yarn around the front of the needle.

3 Pull the yarn down with your index finger.

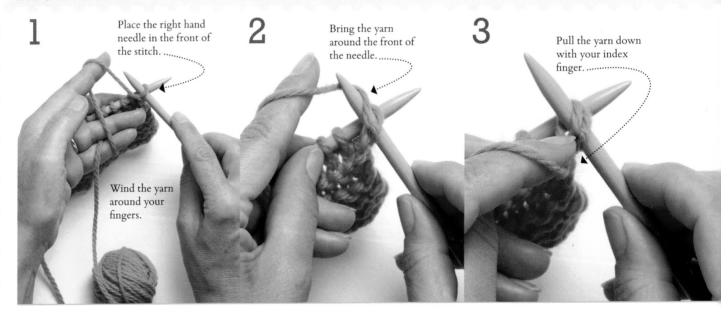

Purl stitch + Knit stitch = Stocking stitch

STOCKING STITCH isn't an actual stitch at all. Instead it is made by working a knit row then a purl row, a knit row then a purl row and so on. The result is a smooth front to the knitting and a "bobbly" back.

FRONT
The knit-stitch side

BACK
The purl-stitch side

4 Pull on the yarn and move the needle from front to back ...

5 ... taking the stitch with it. ...

6 Take the rest of the yarn off the needle to complete the stitch....

Begin the next stitch as in step 1.

4 Bring the right hand needle from front to back taking the yarn with it. ......

5 Pull the rest of the stitch off the needle. ...

6 Now you are ready to begin the next stitch, starting at step 1 again.

Dude dolls

Make an all-in-one doll. Begin by knitting a stripy rectangle. In a few simple steps transform it into a little knitted man.

You will need
• Knitting needles 4mm
• 4 balls of yarn • Soft-toy stuffing
• Tapestry needle

Stop here!
Cast off.

Get started
Work from the bottom changing yarn colour as you move up so each stripe represents a part of the doll's body.

Start here!
Cast on 32 stitches

Hat
Work 10 rows

This colour is part of the 10 rows for the hat.

Head
Work 10 rows – change yarn

Jumper
Work 12 rows – change yarn

Trousers
Work 14 rows – change yarn

Shoes
Work 4 rows – change yarn

Work from shoes to hat

Add felt dots for eyes

How to make the doll

1

Fold the knitting in half so it's inside out.

Sew the edges together.

2

Sew around the top of the knitting and gather it up.

3

Turn the work right side out.

Add the stuffing and sew up the opening.

4

To form the head, sew in a running stitch around the base of the head stripe.

5

Firmly pull on the thread to create a neck.

Add a stitch to make it secure.

6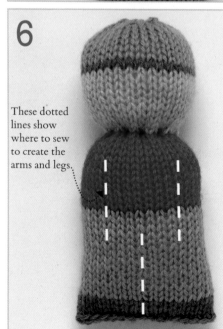

These dotted lines show where to sew to create the arms and legs.

7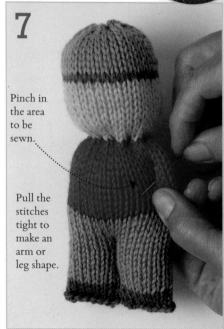

Pinch in the area to be sewn.

Pull the stitches tight to make an arm or leg shape.

Knitted roses

Make a bunch of colourful woolly roses. These simple knitted shapes are twisted and curled to form a rose flower. It only takes a small amount of wool to make one, so it's a neat way of using up spare ends.

You will need

• 4mm knitting needles
• 5m (15ft) of yarn • Felt
• Tapestry needle
• Sewing needle and thread

Rose pattern

Cast on 32 stitches
Row 1: Knit st
Row 2: Purl st
Row 3: Knit st
Row 4: Purl st
Decrease
Row 5: knit two together to end of row =16 st
Row 6: knit two together to end of row = 8 st
Row 7: knit two together to end of row = 4 st
Row 8: knit two together = 2 st
Cast off

How to make a rose

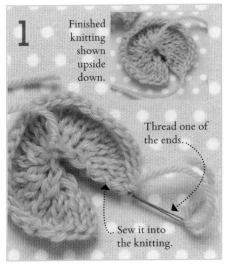

1 Finished knitting shown upside down. Thread one of the ends. Sew it into the knitting.

2 Thread the yarn end from the centre.

3 Turn over the knitting. Twist the knitting into a tight curl to form the rose shape.

4 Sew the outer side of the curl to the back of the rose to hold it in position.

5 Cut out some felt leaves. Sew the leaf to the back of the rose.

Overstitch the edge of the felt with small neat stitches.

Rosy brooch

Your rose makes a pretty brooch. Sew a safety pin to the felt leaves, or sew the roses directly onto your bags; either on their own or in bunches of three.

Knitting braids

Knit some string.
Once you get the hang of it, using a knitting spool is a lot of fun.

You will need

- A variety of colourful knitting yarn (double knit weight is good)
- Knitting spool with pin

How to get started

Thread the yarn through the top of the spool.

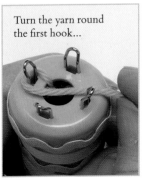

Turn the yarn round the first hook...

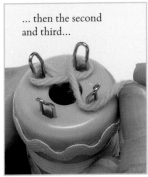

... then the second and third...

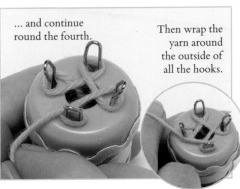

... and continue round the fourth.

Then wrap the yarn around the outside of all the hooks.

Making stitches

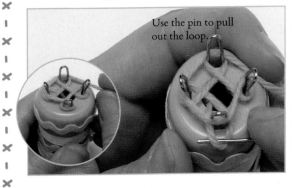

Use the pin to pull out the loop.

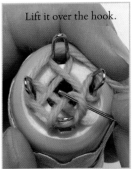

Lift it over the hook.

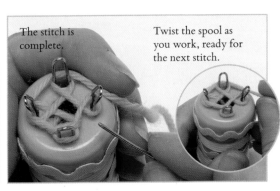

The stitch is complete.

Twist the spool as you work, ready for the next stitch.

Casting off

Take the first stitch off the hook and place it over the hook to the left, make a stitch.

Lift the stitch to the next hook.

Make the last stitch.

Lift up the last stitch and enlarge the loop.

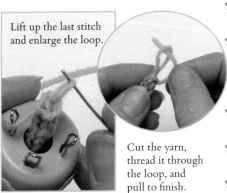

Cut the yarn, thread it through the loop, and pull to finish.

Use long braids about 30cm (12in).

Fold the braid backwards and forward.

Loopy rose

Add green braids to make the leaves.

Sew the loops together in the centre...

Things to make

Braids can be turned into all sorts of fun designs. Try these flower shapes (if you sew on a safety pin you can turn them into brooches).

Tidy the ends away.

Daisy flower

Use about 10 braids 20cm (8in) long....

Tie the braids tightly around their middles....

Curl up a braid and sew it to the middle of the bunch....

Thread the long end on to a needle and thread it down through the braid for about 3cm (1¼in). Pull the needle out and cut off the yarn.

Handy tip

Hold the spool in your left hand and use the pin in the right hand. Twist the spool as you work so the next stitch is facing you. Remember don't knit too tightly.

As the braid grows, pull the end to tighten the work at the top.

Dangly legs and arms

Make us and our dangly arms and legs (see pages 100–103).

The lollipop dolls

Knit a doll, then have fun dressing her and styling her hair. Made up of separate parts, the doll's body is in two colours with a stripe of body colour at the top that makes a ready-made bodice. Her cute, dangly legs are made using a knitting spool.

You will need

- 4mm knitting needles
- Knitting spool • 1m (3ft) yarn for body • 1m (3ft) yarn for skirt
- 50cm (20in) yarn for bodice
- 1m (3ft) yarn for hair
- Knitting spool

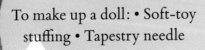

To make up a doll: • Soft-toy stuffing • Tapestry needle

Basic doll pattern

Head • To get the ball shape involves increasing and decreasing. It's the trickiest part of the doll.
Body and bodice • Make up in two colours so it looks like the doll already has clothes on.
Arms and Legs • Use the body colour yarn and a knitting spool.

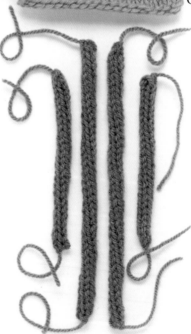

Head

Cast on 4 stitches.
Row 1: Knit 4 st
Row 2: Purl 1 make 1 = 8 st
Row 3: Knit 1 make 1 = 16 st
Row 4: Purl 1 make 1 = 32 st
Row 5–18: continue in stocking stitch, starting with a knit row.
Row 19: Knit 2 together = 16 st
Row 20: Purl 2 together = 8 st
Row 21: Knit 2 together = 4 st
Row 22: Knit 2 together = 2 st
Row 23: Knit 2 together = 1 st
Cast off.

Body and Bodice

Cast on 20 st.
Stocking stitch for 19 rows, starting with knit stitch.
Change colour to body colour.
Stocking stitch for 3 rows in body colour.
Cast off.

Arms and legs

Use a knitting spool (see page 98) and matching yarn.
Knit two 10cm (4in) cords for the arms.
Knit two 18cm (7in) cords for the legs.

Sew on beads for her earrings.

Decorate with buttons to look like jewels.

The stocking stitch skirt will roll up naturally.

Tie the bow at the front or the back.

New clothes
You can mix and match your doll's clothes by changing her skirts and adding more buttons and beads.

Make the head

Use the long ends to sew up the head. Make sure the seam is at the back of the head. Stuff it so it makes a good ball shape.

Turn the knitting inside out.

Using one of the long ends sew up the sides.

Leave an opening for stuffing.

Stuff the head till it feels firm but don't overfill it!

Use the other long end to sew up the hole.

Make the body

Knit the body shape and sew up the sides but remember to move the join to the centre back. Don't overstuff.

Fold the knitting over. Sew the edges together.

Move the join to the centre and sew up the top.

Turn the body the right way out and stuff.

Sew up the opening.

Make the arms and legs

Thread the knitting spool and make the braid the required length. Tidy away one of the ends and leave the other one.

Leave long ends to the braids.

Finish off one end of the braid and leave the other end long.

Cut off yarn.

Put the body together

Once all the body parts are made they are ready to be attached. Sew in place until they are firmly attached.

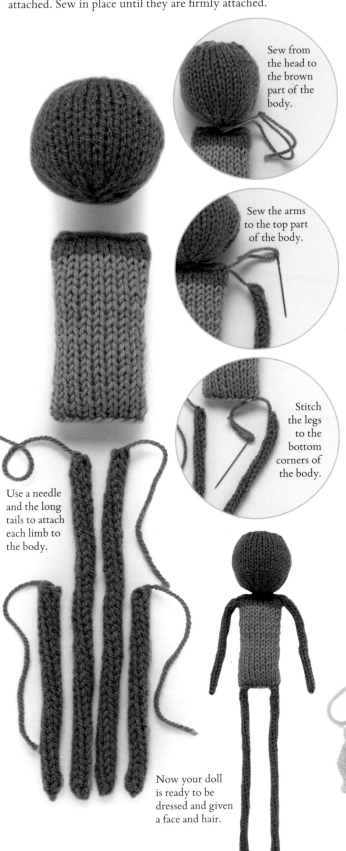

Sew from the head to the brown part of the body.

Sew the arms to the top part of the body.

Stitch the legs to the bottom corners of the body.

Use a needle and the long tails to attach each limb to the body.

Now your doll is ready to be dressed and given a face and hair.

Make the hair

Decide how long the hair should be. Once it is sewn in place it can be styled by cutting it shorter and making a fringe.

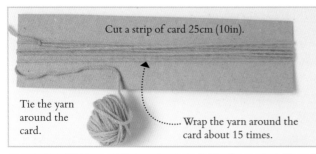

Tie the yarn around the card.

Wrap the yarn around the card about 15 times.

Slide the yarn off the card.

Tie the middle with a short length of yarn.

Secure the hair to the centre of the doll's head.

Sew through the hair end back into the head 4 times.

Make the face

Knot the end of a short length of yarn, and push the needle into the side of the head, bringing it out where the eye will be. Make two stitches, then push the needle back out beside the knot.

Cut off the knot and the rest of the yarn.

Repeat these steps for the other eye and the mouth.

Make a skirt

This skirt is gathered at the top to fit the doll's waist, and joined at the back. The "V" pattern is made by knitting in pink and red yarn.

Skirt Cast on 40 st Knit the first row and continue in stocking stitch until the knitting measures 7cm (3in). Cast off.

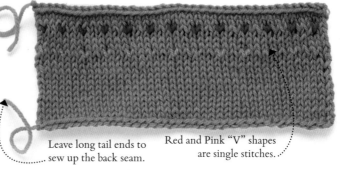

Leave long tail ends to sew up the back seam.

Red and Pink "V" shapes are single stitches.

The red yarn is carried along the row with the blue yarn.

To make the pink and red V shapes, join red yarn to the blue yarn at the beginning of a row. Start knitting with the blue yarn then every fourth stitch use the red yarn instead. At the end of the row, knot the two colours together and cut off the red yarn.

Fold the knitting in half.

Stitch the two sides together.

Sew yarn around the top of the skirt.

Start at the centre front.

Tie the ends into a bow.

Pull the ends of the yarn to gather the skirt.

Stocking stitch will roll up at the edges.

Pom-poms

Jolly pom-poms are really fun to make and make a pretty addition to lots of projects. Sew them to the end of a scarf or use to top off a hat. They're a great way to use up short scraps of yarn – try making multi-coloured balls too.

You will need

Two card discs, 10cm (4in) across

1m (3ft) of yarn, plus 18cm (7in) extra to tie the pom-pom

1

Tie the end of the yarn around the two pieces of card.

Make a slit in both cards.

2

Wind the yarn around and around the discs; the more yarn, the fuller the pom-pom.

3

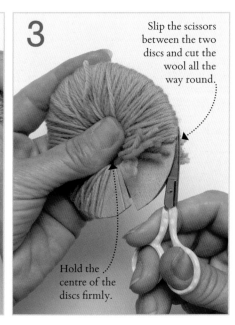

Slip the scissors between the two discs and cut the wool all the way round.

Hold the centre of the discs firmly.

4

Place a 10cm (4in) length of yarn between the card discs.

5

Pull the yarn tight and tie it into a knot.

6

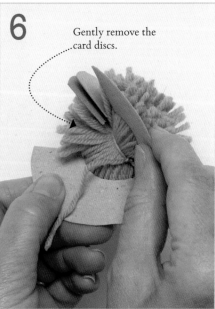

Gently remove the card discs.

Big or small?
To make different-sized pom-poms, simply use bigger or smaller card discs and follow the steps in the same way.

For a really neat shape, snip away the ends of the yarn so they are all the same length.

Use up scraps of yarn that are too short to use for knitting and wrap them around the card.

Crochet

It's all about pulling loops through loops to create a piece of fabric, working with only one stitch at a time – now all you need is a hook and some yarn.

4.5mm crochet hook

8mm crochet hook

Crochet hooks

Hooks are available in many different sizes – the larger the hook, the larger the stitch. The projects that follow are made using a medium-sized 4.5mm hook. Try using a metal hook as the yarn moves more freely compared to a plastic one.

Yarn

The projects in this book are made with cotton yarn in a double knitting (Dk) weight. This cotton yarn is not fluffy like some wools. This makes it perfect for learning how to crochet because it's easy to see the stitches.

Stitch types

When following crochet patterns the stitch names sometimes appear shortened.

Here is a guide:

ch = chain stitch; dc = double crochet (USA = single crochet); htr = half treble (USA = half double crochet); tr = treble (USA= double crochet; ss = slip stitch

Note: some patterns you find elsewhere will be based on USA names, so the results would be very different if the UK name was followed.

How to get started

Working loop

Crochet hook

Stitches

Rows

Unlike knitting, which uses two needles and where the working stitches are all on the needles, crochet is worked with a hook and only one stitch is made at one time.

This has been worked in double crochet.

HOW TO HOLD the work

Wrap the yarn around your left hand as shown here.

Hold the hook in your right hand.

Slip knot   The first stitch on the hook is knotted so the yarn stays on.

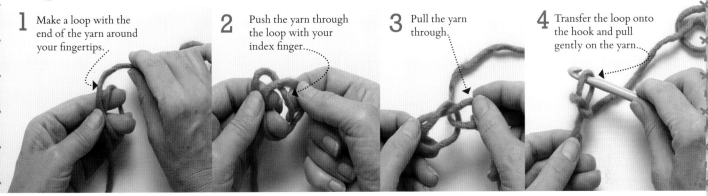

1 Make a loop with the end of the yarn around your fingertips.

2 Push the yarn through the loop with your index finger.

3 Pull the yarn through.

4 Transfer the loop onto the hook and pull gently on the yarn.

Foundation chain   The number of stitches on the chain will determine the width of the crochet fabric.

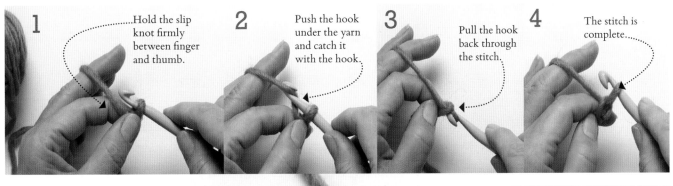

1 ...Hold the slip knot firmly between finger and thumb.

2 Push the hook under the yarn and catch it with the hook.

3 Pull the hook back through the stitch.

4 The stitch is complete...

NOW REPEAT STEPS 1 – 4 to continue the chain.

This foundation chain has 10 stitches – count the "V" shapes.

The back of the stitches will look very bobbly.

Make as many chain stitches as the pattern requires.

1 2 3 4 5 6 7 8 9 10

Double crochet

How to start. Once you have made the foundation chain, you are ready to start crocheting. With any type of stitch you use you will need to make chain stitches at the beginning of each row so that your work is brought up to the right height.

First row in double crochet

Double crochet This basic stitch is useful for all kinds of projects. It produces a close, firm fabric.

Chain stitch At the beginning of the second row make one chain stitch. This means when you begin to work across the row you will begin at the right height.

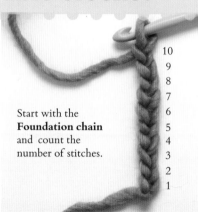

Start with the **Foundation chain** and count the number of stitches.

2 YARN OVER

Push the hook underneath and around the yarn.

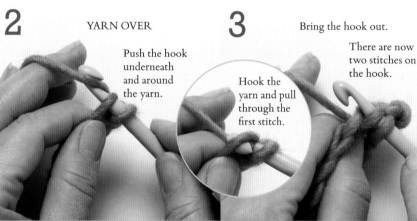

Hook the yarn and pull through the first stitch.

3 Bring the hook out.

There are now two stitches on the hook.

4 Push the hook underneath and around the yarn.

YARN OVER

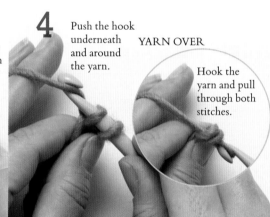

Hook the yarn and pull through both stitches.

Second row in double crochet

(Use this method for all the double crochet rows from now onwards.)

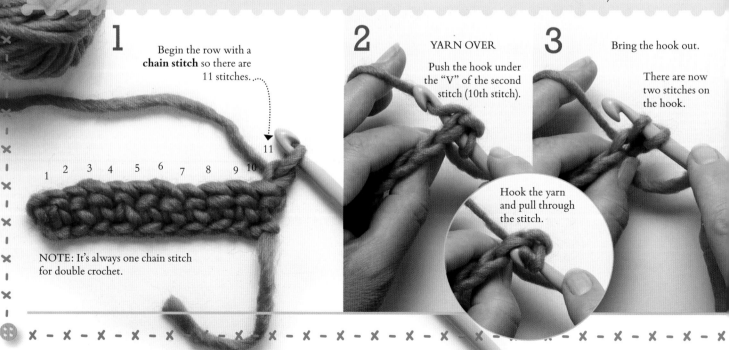

1 Begin the row with a **chain stitch** so there are 11 stitches.

11

1 2 3 4 5 6 7 8 9 10

NOTE: It's always one chain stitch for double crochet.

2 YARN OVER

Push the hook under the "V" of the second stitch (10th stitch).

Hook the yarn and pull through the stitch.

3 Bring the hook out.

There are now two stitches on the hook.

1

At the beginning of Row 1 make a **chain stitch**.

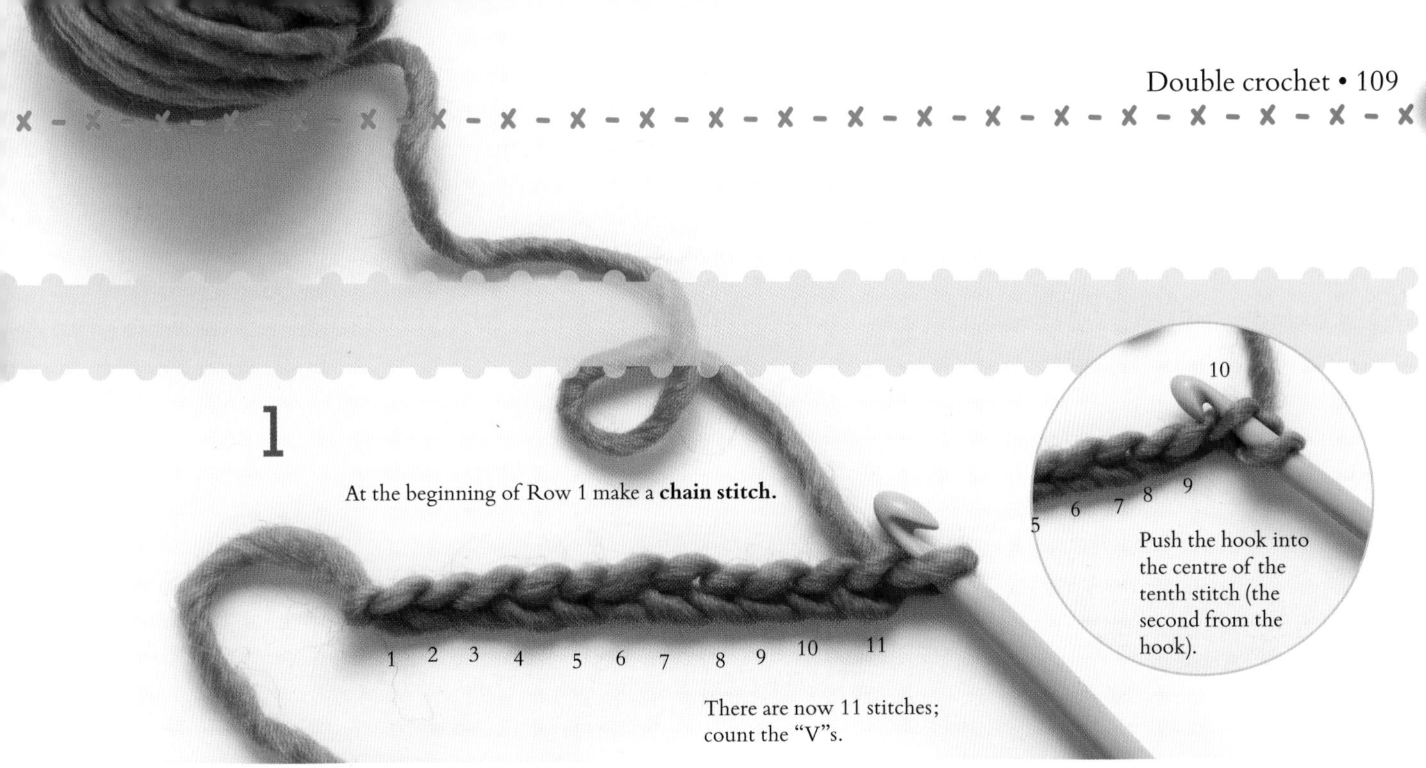

10

5 6 7 8 9

Push the hook into the centre of the tenth stitch (the second from the hook).

1 2 3 4 5 6 7 8 9 10 11

There are now 11 stitches; count the "V"s.

5

Now one stitch is left on the hook.

The **double crochet** stitch is complete.

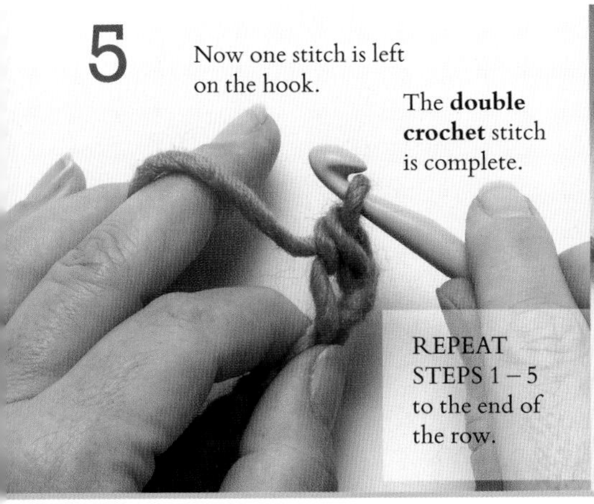

REPEAT STEPS 1 – 5 to the end of the row.

10 9 8 7 6 5 4 3 2 1

The first row is complete - with 10 stitches.

Turn the work to get ready for the next row.

4 YARN OVER

5

The stitch is complete. There is now only one stitch left on the hook.

Hook the yarn and pull through both stitches.

Continue double crochet stitches to the end of the row.

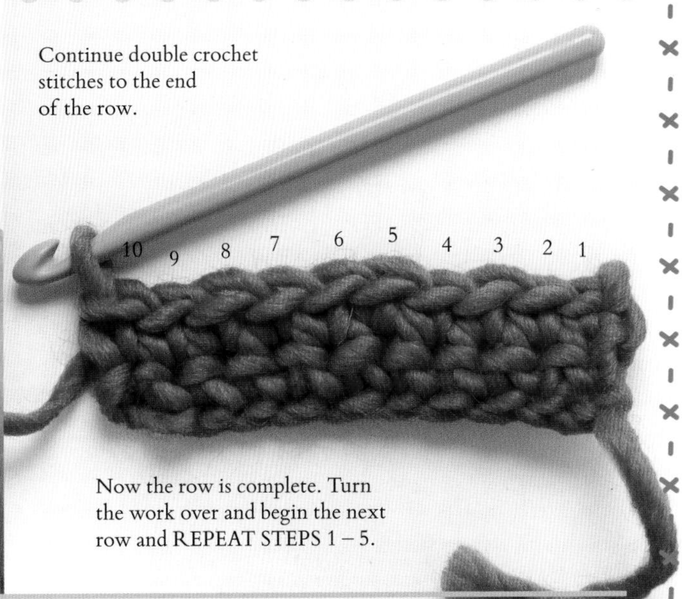

10 9 8 7 6 5 4 3 2 1

Now the row is complete. Turn the work over and begin the next row and REPEAT STEPS 1 – 5.

Crowls

These crocheted owls or "Crowls" are made from a strip of crochet. They make cute little soft toys and even a useful addition to your sewing kit.

You will need
- Cotton yarn for eyes and body
- 4.5mm crochet hook • Soft-toy stuffing • Tapestry needle
- Sewing needle and thread

How to make owls

Small owl body

Foundation chain: 10 stitches. First row: Make 1 chain stitch, double crochet 10 stitches. Continue in double crochet until work measures 18cm (7in) and fasten off.

Owl eyes

Foundation chain: 2 stitches. Double crochet 10 times into the first chain stitch. Slip stitch into the first double crochet stitch and fasten off.

1 Sew in the loose ends. Fold the strip in half. Stitch the sides together.

2 Turn the work inside out.

Stuff the toy, but don't overfill.

3 Sew running stitch around the opening to close it. Pull the thread to gather up the crochet and close the hole.

4 Sew the eye in place with a sewing needle and thread.

Handy tip

Instead of stuffing the owl you can turn it into a handy tape-measure holder. Just pop the tape measure inside and lightly stitch up the opening, checking that the tape measure can run freely in and out.

Small owl

Tape measure

Place tape measure into the opening.

Sew up the opening using overstitch.

Large owl

Foundation chain: 16 stitches.

First row: Make 1 chain stitch, double crochet 16 stitches.

Continue in double crochet until work measures 26cm (10in) and fasten off.

More stitches

The following two stitches produce a different effect to the double crochet. They are taller, which gives them a looser look and they help to give the daisy petals their shape.

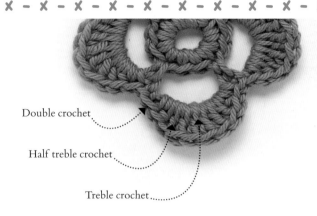

Double crochet

Half treble crochet

Treble crochet

Half treble crochet   (The USA version of this stitch is called "half double crochet".)

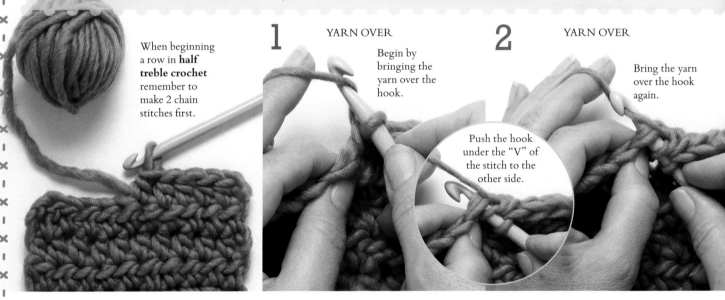

When beginning a row in **half treble crochet** remember to make 2 chain stitches first.

1 YARN OVER

Begin by bringing the yarn over the hook.

Push the hook under the "V" of the stitch to the other side.

2 YARN OVER

Bring the yarn over the hook again.

Treble crochet   (The USA version of this stitch is called "double crochet".)

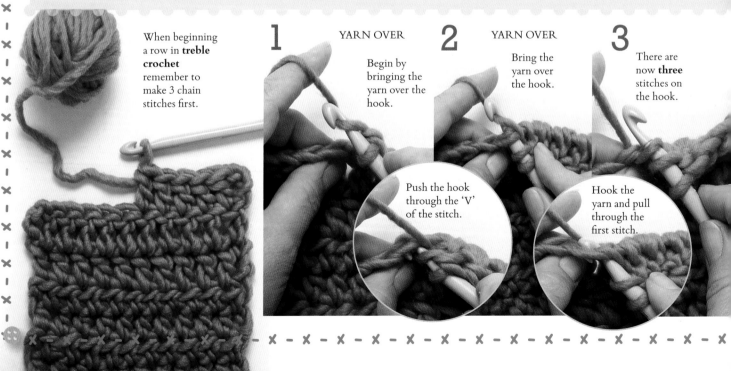

When beginning a row in **treble crochet** remember to make 3 chain stitches first.

1 YARN OVER

Begin by bringing the yarn over the hook.

Push the hook through the 'V' of the stitch.

2 YARN OVER

Bring the yarn over the hook.

Hook the yarn and pull through the first stitch.

3 There are now **three** stitches on the hook.

Turning chains Half treble crochet and treble crochet stitches require a chain stitch at the beginning of a new row, just as double crochet does:

Double crochet = 1 chain stitch
Half treble = 2 chain stitches
Treble crochet = 3 chain stitches

These stitches are needed to bring the end of your work up to the same height as the stitch you are using.

Fasten off

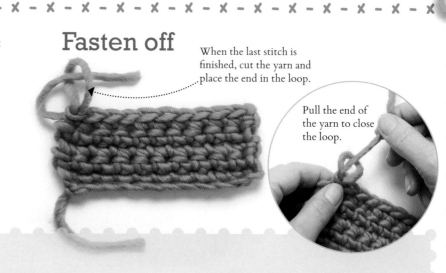

When the last stitch is finished, cut the yarn and place the end in the loop.

Pull the end of the yarn to close the loop.

3 There are now three loops on the hook.

Again, hook the yarn and pull through the stitch.

4 YARN OVER

Bring the yarn over the hook.

Hook the yarn and pull through all three loops.

5 Now one stitch is left on the hook.

This completes the half treble stitch.

REPEAT STEPS 1–5 to the end of the row.

4 YARN OVER

Bring the yarn over the hook.

5 There are now **two** stitches on the hook.

Hook the yarn and pull through the stitch.

6 YARN OVER

Bring the yarn over the hook.

Hook the yarn and pull through both stitches.

7 Now one stitch is left on the hook.

The treble stitch is complete.

REPEAT STEPS 1–7 to the end of the row.

4, 5, or 6 petals
Once you have got the hang of making a four-petalled daisy, try adding more petals by adapting the pattern. Each daisy is made up in three stages and each of these also makes a pretty motif by itself.

A bunch of daisies

These fancy flowers are a perfect way to decorate your clothes and accessories. Create all kinds of variations; from the number of petals to the combination of colours.

Flower brooches can be made by sewing the flowers together and finishing them off with a button.

Hang a daisy from your bag. Simply loop a ribbon around a petal and tie it to the handle.

Top off your hair bands and hats with flowers too. Here the flowers are stitched together, then sewn to the band.

Make a daisy

Make a ring
Make 6 ch to make the circle; ss to the first ch to join the ring.

ch = chain stitch
st = stitch
ss = slip stitch
dc = double crochet
htr = half treble
tr = treble

Make 6 chain stitches.

Slip stitch into the first chain stitch.

The ring is complete.

Round 1
Make 1 ch, then work 12 dc into the ring, then ss into the first ch to join together.

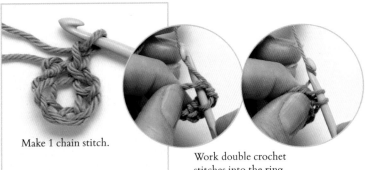

Make 1 chain stitch.

Work double crochet stitches into the ring.

Make 12 double crochet stitches.

Slip stitch into the first chain to join the round.

Round 2
Make 6 ch, ★miss 2 dc; dc into next st, 6 ch; repeat from★ to the end of the round. ss into bottom of first 6ch.

Make 6 chain stitches.

Miss out 2 double crochet and double crochet into the next stitch.

Make 6 chain stitches.

Miss out 2 double crochet and double crochet into the next stitch.

Continue to the end of the round.

Slip stitch into the first chain stitch.

Round 3
★work (1dc, 1htr, 5tr, 1htr, 1dc) into next 6ch space; ss into dc; repeat from ★ to the end of the round.

To make the petal shape crochet a sequence of stitches as follows:

6 chain space.

1 double crochet st
1 half treble stitch
5 treble stitches
1 half treble stitch
1 double crochet st

Work the stitches into the 6 chain space.

Continue around all four petals.

Slip stitch into the double crochet for the first petal.

Crochet patterns

Reading a pattern

can be confusing at first, because all the words and instructions have been shortened. Use the abbreviations to the left as a handy guide to the stitch names.

The symbol ★ works like a bracket. Everything between the ★ symbols is a sequence of stitches that are repeated.

You will need

4.5mm crochet hook • ball of yarn

3 shapes to make

Each round of the daisy makes a cute shape all on its own.

Round 1

Rounds 1 and 2

Rounds 1, 2, and 3

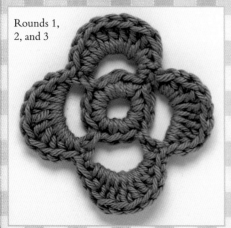

5 and 6 petals

To make more petals simply add more double crochet stitches into the ring as follows.

5 petals Make a ring as before. Round 1: make **15** double crochet stitches into the ring. Round 2: work as usual.

6 petals Make a ring as before. Round 1: make **18** double crochet stitches into the ring. Round 2: work as usual.

Slip stitch (ss)

This stitch is used to join stitches.

With 1 loop on the hook, hook into the next stitch, catch the yarn and pull the loop through the stitch and loop in one movement.

One stitch left on hook.

Make a brooch

Layer up the flowers and sew them together.

Attach a button to the centre.

Sew a safety pin to the back of the flower.

Stitch over and over the back of the pin to secure it.

Bags of stripes

Changing colours is a fun way to liven up a simple strip of double crochet. A length of crochet is useful for lots of projects; here it's a handy bag.

You will need

- Cotton yarn in various colours • 4.5mm crochet hook
- Tapestry needle • Button

How to change colours

Crochet to the end of the row. Turn the work as usual, then cut off the old yarn leaving a tail about 10cm (4in) long. Loop the new colour over the hook leaving a tail about 10cm (4in) long and pull it through the loop on the hook to make a stitch. Tug on the ends to pull the yarn tight. Continue working in new colours. Start the first stitch as chain stitch.

This row is worked in treble crochet.

Remember to chain 3 stitches at the start of the row.

Tidy up the loose ends by sewing them along the edge of the work.

Thread the ends onto the tapestry needle.

BAG PATTERN

Foundation chain: 16 stitches.
Row 1: Make 1 chain stitch, work 16 stitches in double crochet.
Continue working rows in double crochet, changing colours to create stripes.
In this design the stripes are 3 to 4 rows deep, but the number of stripes is up to you. This length of crochet measures 30cm (12in).

Fold the work over, leaving room at the top for the flap.

Stitch the two edges together using overstitch.

Sew up both sides and turn the work inside out.

This row is worked in treble crochet.

Cut a piece of yarn 10cm (4ins).

MAKE A BUTTON LOOP
Push the hook through the crochet, loop the yarn over the hook and pull the hook back through the crochet.
Finish the loop and sew on the button.

Place the ends through the loop and tie a knot to create a loop for the button.

Balls of yarn
Here is a collection of cotton yarn, double-knit (DK) weight. To make the stripe bag, use up leftover lengths.

Templates

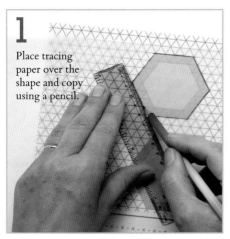

1 Place tracing paper over the shape and copy using a pencil.

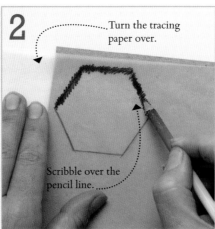

2 Turn the tracing paper over.

Scribble over the pencil line.

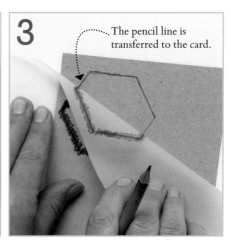

3 The pencil line is transferred to the card.

Transferring designs

Follow steps 1–3 to transfer the patchwork designs onto paper or card.

THE BIRD AND CUP CAKE MOTIFS Because these designs aren't symmetrical, trace the shape on both sides at step one. This way when the paper is turned over the design will be the right way round.

Large cushion
Six-sided cushion, pages 58–59

Triangle patchwork
Squares and triangles, pages 56–57

Small pin cushion
Six-sided cushion, pages 58–59

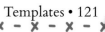

Cup cake

Cup cake motif, pages 70–71

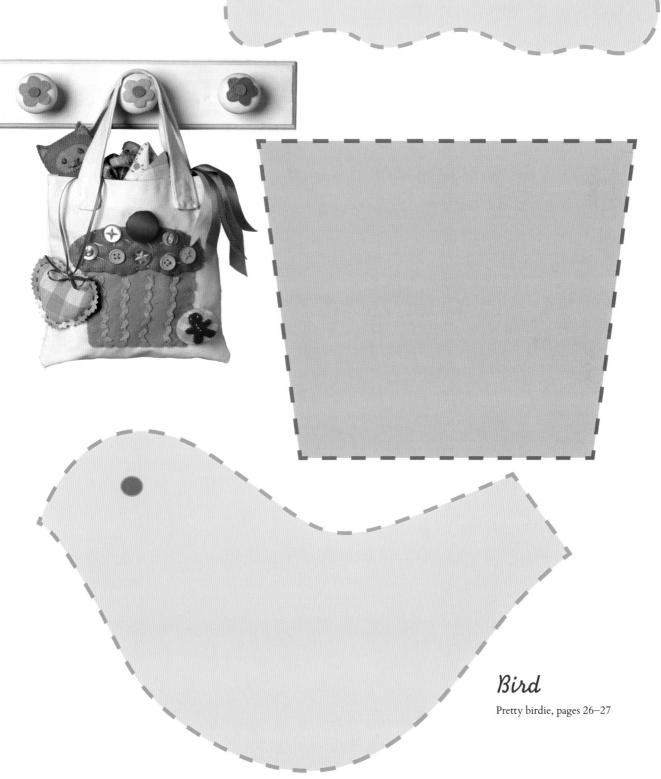

Bird

Pretty birdie, pages 26–27

Stitching patterns

Patterns for picture stitches on pages 32–33 and pixel pictures on pages 44–45.

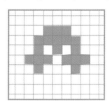

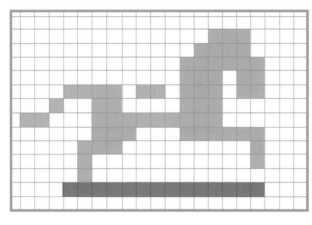

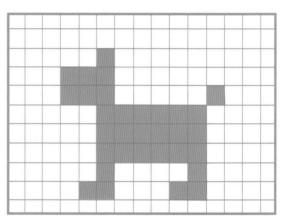

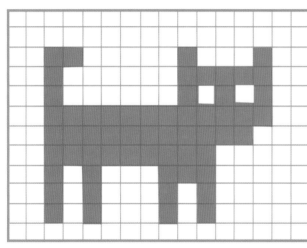

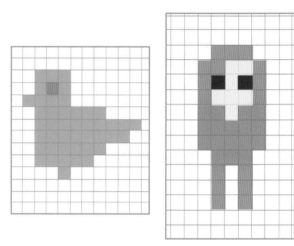

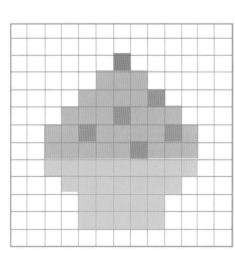

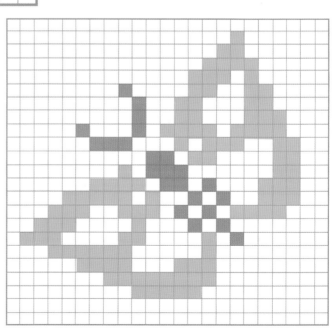

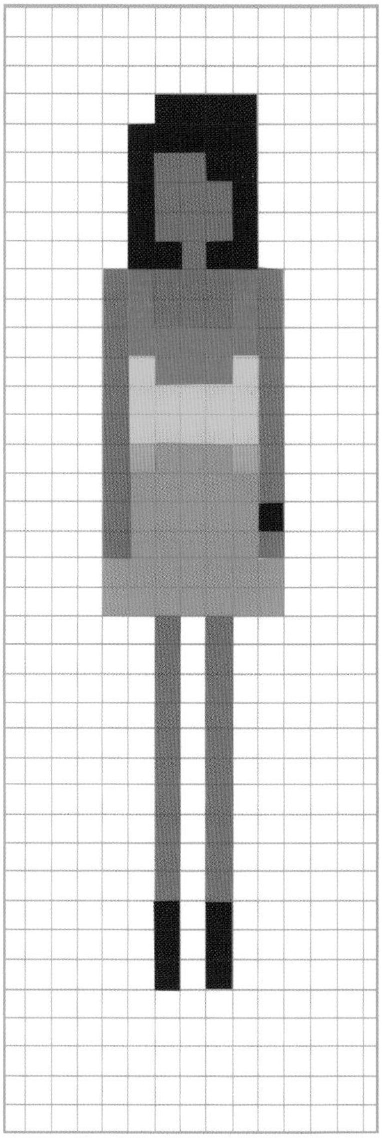

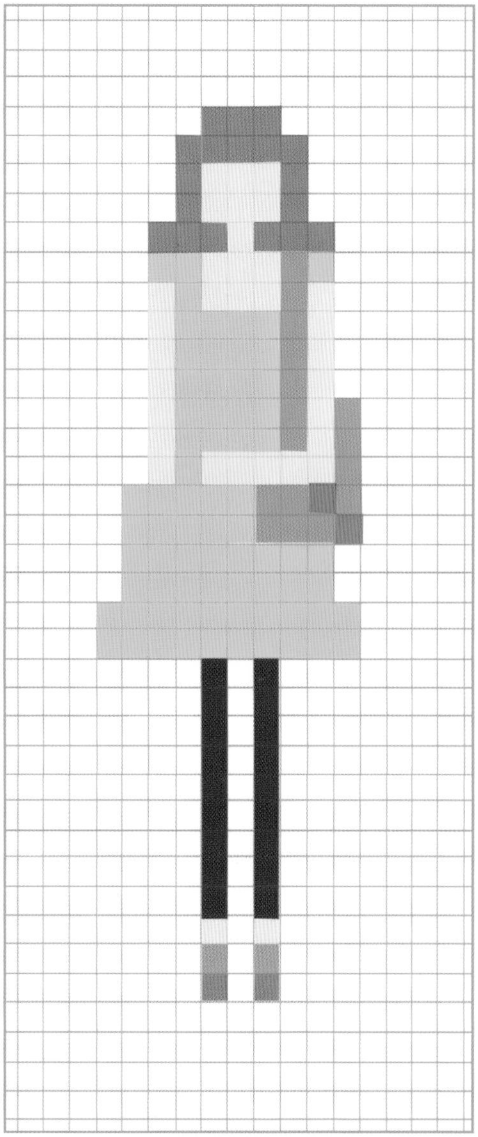

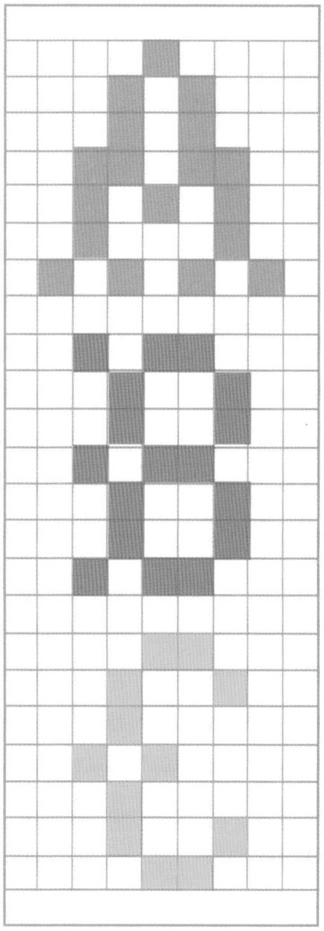

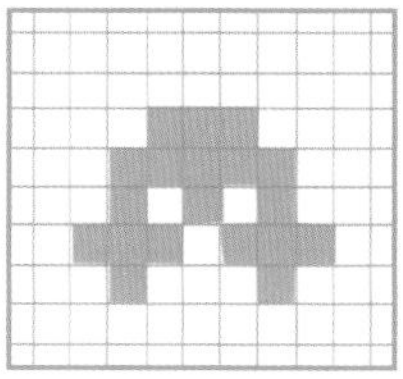

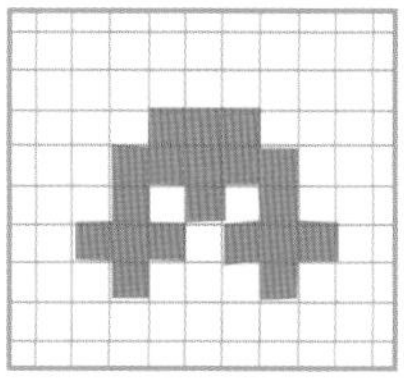

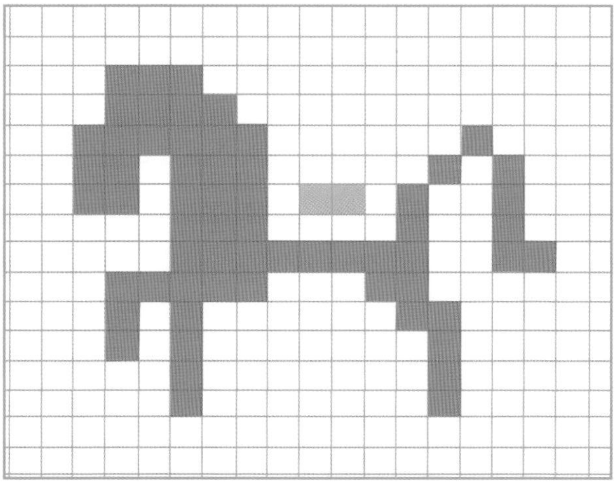

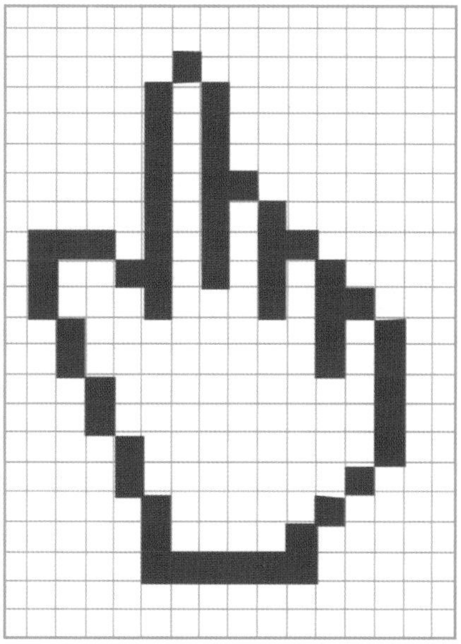

Index

Acknowledgements

Dorling Kindersley would like to thank:
Gemma Fletcher and Rosie Levine for design assistance;
David Fentiman for editorial assistance; Penny Arlon for
proofreading; Ray Williams for production help.

All images © Dorling Kindersley
For further information see: www.dkimages.com